GOD'S CLEANSING STREAM

DELIVERANCE IN THE LOCAL CHURCH

CHRIS HAYWARD

WAGNER
PUBLICATIONS

God's Cleansing Stream
Copyright © 2003 by Chris Hayward
ISBN 1-58502-035-4
Library of Congress Control Number: 2003104972

Published by
Wagner Publications
11005 N. Highway 83
Colorado Springs, CO 80921
www.wagnerpublications.org

Cover design by
Imagestudios
100 East St. Suite 105
Colorado Springs, CO 80903
719-578-0351 www.imagestudios.net

Edit by Christi Goeser
Interior design by Rebecca Sytsema

Rights for publishing this book in other languages are contracted by Gospel Literature International (GLINT). GLINT also provides technical help for the adaptation, translation, and publishing of Bible study resources and books in scores of languages worldwide. For further information, contact GLINT, P.O. Box 4060, Ontario, CA 91761-1003, USA. You may also send e-mail to glintint@aol.com, or visit their web site at www.glint.org.

1   2   3   4   5   6   7   8   9   09   08   07   06   05   04   03

Dedicated to

THE LOCAL PASTOR

Contents

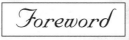

NO HALF MEASURES

This book is being published at a historic juncture in which two notable wars have been engaged. The first is in the Middle East, where a coalition of international forces has confronted the oppression of a nation by a murderous dictator. The second is in every nation on earth, where the multinational Body of Christ is warring to liberate souls from satanic bondage. The former is a political/military struggle conducted very visibly before the eyes of the world. The latter is a spiritual battle, of a reality too seldom appreciated by the world, and at a dimension too seldom fully perceived even among those of us who seek to advance God's redemptive plan for humankind.

The possibilities for analogy between these visible and invisible wars seem endless. They are both profoundly real, and the visible war offers multiple points of parallel with the invisible one—means by which the nature of wars in the military arena might teach principles of spiritual warfare, either by comparison or contrast. As you open the pages of this book, allow me to point out only one—the issue of applying the full dimensions of intended victory that Christ offers those who call on Him as Savior and Lord.

NO HALF MEASURES

When declaration of attack was made at the onset of the war against Iraq in March, 2003, the leader of the coalition said, "There will be no half measures." With these words, he was addressing the fact that 12 years before, that nation was driven back from expansionist efforts against neighboring states, but no full-dimensioned victory was pursued, and no complete application of victory applied. The result was the resurfacing of evil's face in human affairs, bringing about the need at this time to break the back of the enemy. The new objective was announced: This time there will be the complete deliverance of peoples from their oppressor, not only a rescuing of a people from an intruder. This contemporary picture clearly illustrates the point of this book—and a point about the multiple dimensions of salvation's provision in Christ.

When Jesus Christ declared, "It is finished" from His Cross, in three words He asserted that Calvary had accomplished no "half measures." There is no question as to the Master's triumph of *"that serpent of old called the Devil and Satan"* (Rev. 12:9), whose dominion has been taken from him—but who yet succeeds wherever the Truth is hidden or rejected, and thus his lies succeed.

Still, notwithstanding what Jesus has achieved, "half measures" still exist in much of the life of His Church. They survive wherever the *promise* of forgiveness of sin and the hope of eternal life is proclaimed, but where the *provision* of full deliverance and joy in believing is untaught or unknown.

The full scope of "deliverance" is announced in 2 Corinthians 1:10—*"[God] delivered us from so great a death, and does de-*

liver us; in whom we trust that He will still deliver us." Saving faith is given not only to *birth* us unto life by God's *justifying* grace, but to *liberate* us from sin's residual dynamic through His *sanctifying* grace. This book is a powerful resource to help Jesus' whole Church better see the fuller provisions given us, and to cultivate sensible, sensitive disciples who not only know its benefits in their own lives, but who will grow to minister its grace to others.

A WORTHY WORK

You have in hand a worthy work—not only worthy in its content, biblical substance, and spiritual mission, but also authored by a worthy brother-in-Christ. My acquaintance with Chris Hayward is deep, and his track record of fidelity to a Bible-based, Christ-exalting lifestyle and ministry is well proven. I have complete confidence in both his integrity and his practical wisdom, and I commend his character and teaching to you; attesting to his trustworthiness as a servant of Jesus as surely as I would to his faithfulness as a husband and father. As he presents you with insight into a demanding and potentially confusing subject, he clearly gives an undeniably sound-minded, biblical foundation for everything he offers. Chris also puts the matter squarely on the table where it belongs: he shows "deliverance ministry" as a central part of Christian discipleship, not as some specialized art form supposedly only for the spiritually arcane!

In scores of audio teachings, as well as my writing on this subject, I have always opposed the idea that ministry involving the demonic ever become sensationalized. With this strong stance, you will find here nothing of a cheap sideshow to titillate the tastes of the mystically inclined. Rather, you will find help toward fully responding to Jesus, the Lord of the Church, Who said, *"These signs shall follow them that believe ... they shall cast out demons"*

(Mark 16:17). His plan for His Church not only is full-measured in its provision through the Cross, but calls us to full measures in discipling those who come to Him there. Being discipled to bring people *unto faith in Christ* is unquestionably our priority; but failing to lead people *unto freedom through Christ* is to deal in "half measures." That is why I so heartily commend this book—and Cleansing Stream Ministries (CSM)—which it presents as the functional resource which it has already become in so many places around the world. The central focus of both—this book and CSM—is *discipleship;* seeing people who *know* the Savior, who learn to *overthrow* the enemy, and who begin to *show* others the path to matching their faith in Jesus with the freedom He has provided for them through the Cross. Again—as I have said—all of this is so very, very worthy.

Yes, political and military battles do come and go across our war-weary earth, but all analogy that would parallel their coming and going with the spiritual warfare in which we are engaged ends at that point. The reason? Because the spiritual battle never "goes"—it is ongoing and will be until the King returns for His bride and this present age is swallowed up in the ages to come. And until then, dear ones, we are called to "do business"—full-measured Kingdom business like Jesus said, describing our mandate as His servants (Luke 19:13). So by God's grace, may this handbook serve to help you do that, so that we all together may serve the Savior's "business plan" more completely and effectively until the last battle is fought—when we will celebrate the final triumph at His appearing.

Jack W. Hayford, Chancellor
The King's College and Seminary
The Church On The Way
Van Nuys, California

Acknowledgments

Fifteen years prior to joining the staff of Cleansing Stream Ministries (CSM), I attended the yearly Autumn Leadership Conferences hosted by Dr. Jack Hayford. It was here that crucial concepts of pastoring were formed. He continues to make an indelible impact on my life. If it were not for C. Peter Wagner's friendship and gentle prodding to begin this project, it would still be merely an idea. He is a unique combination of time-tested, godly wisdom and youthful exuberance. I am increasingly aware of how much our individual accomplishments depend upon the hard work and expertise of others. This is a relatively small book, yet I found myself at an impasse on a number of occasions. The excellent editing provided by Christi Goeser along with her encouraging words helped open the way and make this book possible. Under the watchful, diligent eye of CSM Project Manager, Gail Shipp, clarity, definition, and consistency came into focus. My dear friend Joy Dawson provided invaluable advice to protect the integrity of this message and to keep it on track. Finally and most importantly, my wife, Karen, was and continues to be a source of tremendous encouragement and inspiration.

Part One

THE
FOUNDATION
FOR
DELIVERANCE

Chapter One

A TEAR IN THE GARMENT

*No one puts a piece of unshrunk cloth on an old
garment; for the patch pulls away from the
garment, and the tear is made worse.*

MATTHEW 9:16

It's hard to say when the idea of evil first became a part of my understanding of the world around me. As a child, I experienced the normal chills and thrills of shapeless monsters under my bed and bogeymen lurking amongst the ominous shadows on my moon-lit wall—forcing me to bury my head beneath the covers and pray to fall asleep quickly! As I grew up, many of these fears were doused by rational thought. I could convince myself that evil wasn't really a physical force. Evil was merely "bad thoughts," easily overcome by intelligent reason.

It wasn't until I became an adult that I realized my childhood perceptions weren't as foolish as I had been led to believe. Evil *was* real, but it was more than vague shadows on a wall. Evil was the reality of demonic presence loosed in Earth because of sin, seeking to thwart the plan of God, hoping to waylay His people and bring them down.

Jesus affirmed that demons do exist. The apostles bore witness to this as well; centuries of Church history also bear that out. And any honest person would look at the atrocities committed around the world today and agree that their root goes far beyond what mortal mind can scheme. Demons inspire works of darkness, inciting people to acts that cause harm. Demons are real and they labor for no other reason than to steal, kill, and destroy (see John 10:10).

As a Christian minister, it has been my privilege to see thousands of people released from demonic assault. Over and over again I have seen the power of Jesus Christ lead willing hearts to freedom they never thought they'd enjoy. Unfortunately, such deliverance is sometimes misunderstood, even railed against, as demonic in and of itself. I can't count the times I've heard a pastor tell me stories of wild abuse in the area of Christian deliverance ministry. And it grieves me, because I know it grieves the heart of God. Evil is real, but so is the power of Jesus Christ—and He wants His people free!

This book is born out of a desire to shine light upon the often clouded subject of deliverance. The Bible speaks plainly about deliverance ministry; in fact, it is a part of Jesus' clarion announcement of the arrival of the kingdom of God. He came to destroy the works of the devil and because of the reality of the presence of evil in our world every person needs to experience this deliverance (see Luke 11:20; Acts 10:38; Hebrews 2:14-15; 1 John 3:8).

"I believe in deliverance, I just don't believe in deliverance ministries." This statement, or one similar, is not uncommon among pastors. Over the past several years I have spoken to hundreds of pastors and leaders who share the same concern. They recognize that there are spiritual and emotional needs among many of those they serve that exceed what can be met through psychological counseling. Yet, these pastors' experiences with deliverance ministries have for the most part been disastrous. Things have taken place in the name of deliverance that never ought to have happened, from truly unbiblical practices to goofy and downright absurd. No wonder pastors are cautious.

Consequently, because of poorly handled deliverance ministry, there is a tear, or hole, in the garment of the Church. People haven't understood the freedom God wants to bring to them and haven't experienced it in its fullness. There is still too much bondage among God's people. So what do we do? Where do we go from here? If we try to patch this tear with something new and untried, we will only further damage the entire garment. So what do you do when there is a tear in the garment? The likelihood of finding another bolt of exact fabric to match the age, color, and pattern of the torn garment is remote. If, however, you take a piece from the inside hem of the original, it can be done. God has given us His plan for this vital ministry, and He is bringing it back into balance, mending the tear with threads of grace and material of sound doctrine.

THE EARLY CHURCH

Deliverance is not a new idea. The Church has been experiencing God's power to deliver since its inception. In particular, the first century Church was quite accustomed to casting out demons. Ancient writings unilaterally confirm that deliverance from demonic bondage was widespread among believers in the Early Church. During the first and second centuries, Christian writers such as Lactantius and Cyril of Jerusalem spoke of deliverance as a continuing practice. Christian orators and teachers such as Justin Martyr, Tertullian, and Origin verify through their personal testimonies that Christians were active in their prayers and ministry to those needing deliverance from demonic bondage. Deliverance was so common a part of church life that when the apostate Emperor Julian wanted to satirize the Christian community, he taunted that two things marked the essence of their belief and ministry: driving out demons and making the sign of the Cross.

Interestingly, making the sign of the Cross was a key part of driving evil powers away. Why? Because the Cross spoke of all God did to effectively and completely destroy the works of darkness. The Cross is the paramount defeat of Satan. And it is clear that driving out demons and their dark works of bondage formed an important, if not primary, function of the Church. These radical followers of Christ, ignited by the freedom they themselves had experienced, sang psalms, spoke the name of Jesus, quoted Scripture, laid hands on the sick, gave money to the poor, prayed, and fasted to see others come to know the liberty and peace of living under God's rule.

Where did this prayer and deliverance happen? Lest we think it was a behind-closed-doors ministry, consider the following fact: There was a special office within the church specifically for deliverance. Those appointed to serve were prepared by special training and served on the staff alongside presbyters, deacons, and others. They were in the middle of church life, held accountable, and esteemed. The third-century congregation at Rome, for example, employed fifty-two ministers to cast out demons.

Deliverance was more than entertainment or spiritual hype. It was a part of the experience of being saved and brought into the Christian community. At the time of the Early Church, society was so saturated with demonic influences through pagan worship and immorality that those who wished to receive baptism and join the Church were expected to undergo a number of deliverance experiences to cleanse them spiritually.[1]

The conclusion of this book is in keeping with the views of these Early Church leaders. They did not see the need for deliverance as a toggle switch that is either on or off. It was not a matter of the new believer being either "possessed" or "free." Rather, the succession of deliverance experiences was to break the grip of demons from successive areas of one's life as they were addressed in the discipleship process.

THE LOCAL CHURCH

There are well over six hundred references in the Old and New Testaments to the words "deliverance," "delivered," or "deliver." Interestingly, the vast majority of these Scriptures are addressed to God's people—not to the unbeliever. The first and greatest deliverance comes to us when we receive Jesus Christ as Lord and Savior. We read in Colossians 1:13: *"He has **delivered** us from the power of darkness and conveyed us into the kingdom of the Son of His love"* (emphasis added). An ever-increasing number of pastors are seeking help in bringing God's deliverance to their flock. They recognize that once a person is saved a great amount of work still lies ahead. Sanctification is a process and it often comes with great conflict. The transforming work of the Holy Spirit is usually met with resistance and that resistance often can be demonic. You may be thinking, *But wasn't the devil defeated at the Cross? Wasn't his head crushed?* The answer is Yes! He was defeated and has been stripped of authority (i.e., a crushed head). But the devil is still the father of lies, and he is still the rebellious leader of a demonic structure. He roams the earth like a roaring lion seeking whom he might devour (see 1 Peter 5:8). We, the children of God, have been granted authority over him and his works through the redemptive work of Jesus Christ. God granted us the authority to use His name in advancing the kingdom of God and to defeat the works of darkness (see Matthew 16:19; Luke 10:19). Think of it this way: an officer of the law has been given authority to exercise power according to the law. Criminals don't stop their lawless acts simply because there are police. The police must use their authority to apprehend and bring criminals to justice.

God gave the Promised Land to Abraham and his descendants, the future Hebrew nation. After a marvelous deliverance from Egyptian bondage, Joshua took them across the Jordan River to claim their land—but it was not won without considerable warfare.

Somehow in God's wonderful order, He uses the prayers of His people as a restraint against demonic activity, inviting the presence of God to intervene in the course of human events.

Though the land was theirs, they had to possess it. This call to war wasn't something they would have to manage alone. God spoke reassuringly, *"Little by little I will drive them out from before you, until you have increased, and you inherit the land"* (Exodus 23:30). Likewise, deliverance must not be looked at as a once-in-a-life-time event, but as part of the sanctification process. An individual can be instantly set free from a particular bondage by the power of God. However, he or she, while in this earthly body, is meant to continue advancing in Christlikeness. The Lord had given the entire land of promise to His children today too, but they must take possession of it *"little by little...lest the beasts of the field become too numerous for you"* (vv. 29-30).

God will not allow us to take back ground that we cannot maintain. We must occupy what He has given us to possess. So great is the promise of God, that He will contend with our enemies until they are destroyed (see Deuteronomy 7:22-23)! As we advance to drive out the enemy in our lives there will be warfare. Yet, *"the Lord your God, the great and awesome God, is among you."* (v. 22) and He *"will inflict defeat upon them until they are destroyed"* (v. 23). Amen! What hope!

So how does deliverance apply to Christians? The Bible says, *"Do not give the devil a foothold"* (Ephesians 4:27, NIV). The word "foothold" in the Greek is *topos*, from which we derive the English word "topography." As Christians, it is possible to give demons a place in our lives. Having been under Satan's rule before we came to Christ, we are comfortable with a certain amount of evil. But when we experience the life-changing power of salvation, it takes us out of the darkness and gives us a new inheritance. Like the Hebrew people of old discovered, the land—our lives—is legally ours, but it needs a bit of clearing out! The Holy Spirit, through the Word of God, opens our eyes and we embrace truth, repent, and reject the lies. Armed with His truth and authority, we can cast the enemy off our land.

WHAT ARE DEMONS?

"And when He had come out of the boat, immediately there met Him out of the tombs a man with an unclean spirit, who had his dwelling among the tombs; and no one could bind him, not even with chains, because he had often been bound with shackles and chains. And the chains had been pulled apart by him, and the shack-

les broken in pieces; neither could anyone tame him. And always, night and day, he was in the mountains and in the tombs, crying out and cutting himself with stones" (Mark 5:2-5).

A demon is a fallen angel. When Satan rebelled against God, he took a large number of the angels with him (see Isaiah 14:12-15; Revelation 12:3,4). When their rebellion failed, they were cast out of heaven (see Luke 10:18). Those angels are now recognized as demons. Demons reach the depths of hatred, bitterness, and perversion. They hate all that is God's purpose, intent, or works—most notably humankind. Demons hate people because they are God's masterpiece. They torment and harass people, leading them away from God and His truth (see Mark 5: 2-5; Acts 13:6-12). Although lust, homosexuality, drunkenness, gluttony, and witchcraft are expressions of sinful flesh, these are among practices that can also be expressions of demonic activity in the lives of people. Somehow in God's wonderful order, He uses the prayers of His people as a restraint against demonic activity, inviting the presence of God to intervene in the course of human events.

WHAT POWER DO CHRISTIANS HAVE OVER DEMONS?

"He who is in you is greater than he who is in the world" (1 John 4:4).

The Christian believer, by having the Holy Spirit within, has power over all demons. When Jesus Christ sent His disciples out on their mission, He said He was giving them authority over all the power of the enemy (see Luke 10:19). Jesus' authority is greater than all satanic power. *"When the disciples said, 'Lord, even the demons are subject to us in Your name.' Jesus replied, 'Do not rejoice in this, that the spirits are subject to you, but rather rejoice because your names are written in heaven'"* (Luke 10:17,20). The

Christian believer has unlimited authority over demons in the name of Jesus. That authority, however, is nothing compared to the blessings of salvation, the indwelling power of the Holy Spirit, and the glory we will know in heaven.

CAN A CHRISTIAN BE DEMON-POSSESSED?

"When an unclean spirit goes out of a man, he goes through dry places, seeking rest; and finding none, he says, 'I will return to my house from which I came' And when he comes, he finds it swept and put in order. Then he goes and takes with him seven other spirits more wicked than himself, and they enter and dwell there; and the last state of that man is worse than the first" (Luke 11:24-26).

Deliverance is the act of casting a demon out of the place given to it by a person. It is possible for an unbeliever to be occupied by one or more demons (see Luke 11:24-26). Through true repentance and an encounter with the power of the Holy Spirit, that person can be delivered from demonic bondage. Having been *"swept clean"* (v. 25), they must receive Jesus Christ or face the possibility of greater demonic bondage (v. 26). However, once an individual receives Jesus Christ as Savior and Lord, the Holy Spirit makes His abode within. That person's spirit, having been made alive through rebirth, then becomes the dwelling place of the Holy Spirit.

Once possessed by the Holy Spirit, a Christian cannot be possessed in their *spirit* by a demon. Their *soul* (i.e., mind, will, and emotions) can, however, be demonically harassed in many ways and with varying degrees of torment. These attacks from demons can be initiated because of personal trials (see 2 Corinthians 12:7), by believing the lies of the enemy (see 2 Corinthians 10:4-6), or by engaging in sinful activity (see Ephesians 4:27).

When speaking of Christians and the demonic, "possession" is the wrong word. Some prefer "demonized." At times these theological disagreements are nothing more than splitting hairs over word usage. The real issue is this: Is it possible for a Christian to be tempted, tormented, harassed, and influenced by demons? Is it possible for a Christian to embrace deception to the point where he or she relinquishes control and becomes dominated by the deceiver? I believe the answer to these questions is yes. The other reality is that this comes in varying stages and degrees of intensity. Peter, when rebuked by Jesus for embracing the lie from Satan that He was to not go to Jerusalem to suffer, die, and be raised again (see Mark 8:31-33), though gravely deceived, was not in as severe bondage as Simon the sorcerer (see Acts 8:18-24, NIV) who "full of bitterness" and "captive to sin," tried to buy the power demonstrated by the apostles.

WHAT ABOUT DELIVERANCE TODAY?

Since the founding of the Church there has always been a remnant that functioned in deliverance. Some have taught and practiced deliverance for years. Jack Hayford has done as much as anyone to shape my life as a pastor. As the founding pastor of The Church on the Way in Van Nuys, California, Dr. Hayford has mentored thousands in the ministry of deliverance, having taught and practiced it for over thirty years. The focus has never been on demons but on God and discipleship of His people. Deliverance was just a part of the normal, balanced life of the church, whose goal was to "grow people."

And through his influence, Cleansing Stream Ministries was born. The Church by and large has neglected this vital ministry, embracing Christian counseling as the answer to emotional and spiritual struggles. While counseling certainly has its place, it is generally not equipped to deal with demonic harassment or ... tually rooted problems.

While my particular vision and burden is to see the deliverance ministry under the umbrella of the local church, I want to make clear that there are proven parachurch organizations operating effectively in the areas of deliverance. My deep desire is that the local church be fully equipped to bring every believer into the freedom for which Christ paid the price for them to experience. Unfortunately, the deliverance ministry has often been neglected in that pursuit. Instead of a few having some "secret" understanding of spiritual warfare and casting out demons, it is my belief that every disciple should be filled and anointed by the Holy Spirit to continue doing as Jesus did: *"Preach the gospel to the poor...heal the brokenhearted...proclaim liberty to the captives and recovery of sight to the blind...set at liberty those who are oppressed ...proclaim the acceptable year of the LORD"* (Luke 4:18-19).

The thought of a church full of people equipped and functioning in such a manner can be scary for many pastors, especially when viewing it through the lens of the past where wrong teachings, attitudes, and behaviors have too often prevailed. Many are apprehensive to allow people to lay hands on others to pray for them, let alone to cast out demons. For these hesitant leaders, it is not a hard stretch to imagine a chaotic mess ending in a reputation for being the weirdest church in town. But, what if it were done decently and in order? What if it could be established scripturally and maturely?

That is what this book is all about. Thousands of pastors and churches in the United States and around the world have discovered that this necessary ministry can function in the local church with great success. As president of Cleansing Stream Ministries, a worldwide discipleship ministry, I can say that this is our mission.

As an overview, our ministry provides two seminars which are to be conducted in the local church led by and under the covering of pastoral leadership: (1) The Cleansing Stream Seminar, which prepares the participant to *receive deliverance,* at the Regional Retreat, through discipleship in basic truths and disciplines and (2) The Cleansing Stream Discipleship Seminar, which prepares the participants to *minister deliverance* as a team in the local church and with Cleansing Stream at Regional Retreats, in submission and order.

The Cleansing Stream Seminar is a 12-week seminar plus a Retreat; that can be open to anyone in the congregation. Its contents are as follows:

- Session #1: Walk in the Spirit
- Session #2: Commit Everything to God
- Session #3: Speak Words of Life
- Session #4: Enter the Cleansing Stream
- Regional Retreat (where the seminar participants receive ministry)
- Session #5: Press Toward the Goal

The Cleansing Stream Discipleship Seminar requires a two-year training commitment, including ministering at retreats and team prayer in the local church. It is open to those prayerfully chosen by pastoral leadership. It has nine session teachings covering three main steps:

- First Step: Who He is and Who We Are
- Second Step: The Weapons of Our Warfare
- Third Step: Yes, You're An Intercessor

Throughout this book I will be referring to the work of Cleansing Stream Ministries, sharing the things we've learned and implemented to strengthen local churches to minister deliverance. I am not saying that we have all the answers, or that we do everything right. But God has poured out His blessing upon us, and we desire to share what He's done. We are committed to partnering with pastors and churches in teaching and training leaders and maturing believers in personal cleansing, deliverance, and spiritual warfare so they can be released to serve, minister, and disciple others in the Body of Christ.

My personal prayer is that every local church in the world will embrace the ministry of deliverance in such a way that it again becomes a natural part of the fabric of the church. Thousands of churches in the United States and around the world have discovered that deliverance within the local church can be as natural as breathing is to the body.

Note

1. For a complete analysis of deliverance in the Early Church, see Dr. Joseph B. Fuiten Hedges, *The Prince of the World will be Driven out: A Comprehensive Biblical Analysis of the Different Types of Activity in the Spiritual Area* (prepared originally as a doctoral dissertation), January 1994, Literature Review 15, Chapter: Paul Thigpen, "Spiritual Warfare in the Early Church," pp.21-23.

Chapter Two

THE GREAT DECEPTION: "IT'S JUST THE WAY I AM!"

*For My people have committed two evils: They
have forsaken Me, the fountain of living waters,
and hewn themselves cisterns—broken cisterns
that can hold no water.*

JEREMIAH 2:13

WHY CAPTIVITY?

There were two reasons why the Israelites, God's chosen people, went into captivity. First, they had forsaken their only hope— the one source of true life that would sustain them throughout their days. The Lord was their provider. He was their protector. It was He who led them to victory over their adversaries. It was He who made a place for them and enriched their lives. Yet they joined themselves with the gods of the land and forsook the Lord. Despite their rejection, He loved them and sent prophets to warn them of the pending disaster that awaits those who give themselves over to worthless things, but they would not listen.

Their second sin was to attempt to fabricate their own blessings, to become self-sufficient consumers who needed no external source for life or subsistence. But by rejecting the Lord, the Israelites had become nothing but broken cisterns. In God's sight they were buckets with holes. Anything of value poured into them would be just as quickly lost. Trying to satisfy their needs themselves, they had become empty people who were dying of thirst. They had refused the fresh water God freely offered.

Amazingly, the story doesn't end there. It was the kindness of God that led them into captivity, because only through captivity would they become aware of the bondage they were in. Only then would they cry out to the Lord, forsake their idols, and be led to freedom. So why captivity? It brings us to our senses and allows God to turn us around and sets us back on the road of freedom and liberty.

An example of this wonderful kind of redeeming love is seen in the book of Hosea. Hosea was a prophet who was told by God to marry an unfaithful woman—a prostitute named Gomer. She was a living illustration of how the Israelites, the chosen bride of God, had treated her intended husband, the Lord. For us today, Gomer, typifies how many of God's people who forsake Him are led into captivity. This captivity is not a punishment as much as it is a door to repentance and, thus, deliverance. Consider the following passage where God speaks about His love for His broken and wayward people:

"Therefore I am now going to allure her; I will lead her into the desert and speak tenderly to her. There I will give her back her vineyards, and will make the Valley of Achor a door of hope. There she will sing as in the days of her youth, as in the day she came up out of Egypt. 'In that day,' declares the LORD, 'you will call me 'my husband;' you will no longer call me 'my master.' I will remove

the names of the Baals from her lips; no longer will their names be
invoked. ...I will betroth you to me forever; I will betroth you in
righteousness and justice, in love and compassion. I will betroth
you in faithfulness, and you will acknowledge the LORD'" (Hosea
2:14-20, NIV).

We can live in captivity, held in bondage to the enemy, and not
even realize it. In the days of Jeremiah and Hosea, the captivity of
His people was physical and tangible. For us, we may not be physically captive, but can walk around just as bound—bound by rejection, shame, impurity, abuse, anger, unforgiveness, self-hatred, and
addictions of all sorts. These bonds can be excused as just quirks
of our personality or deficiencies that we have to put up with until
Jesus comes. Yet these "weaknesses" often have spiritual roots
that cannot be dealt with apart from the delivering power of Jesus
Christ. The devil will run any ground we give him. The few I have
mentioned are causing unprecedented misery within the Body of
Christ even as you read this page. It is not an exaggeration to say
that much of the Church is bound up in these areas.

THE ROADRUNNER MENTALITY

So what are we afraid of? Why is it so difficult for us to admit that
there are areas in our lives that are really messed up? To begin
with, Christians can be deceived by the devil. They can be tempted,
harassed, and tormented by demonic beings. And, given enough
ground, the adversary is able to manipulate and influence the behavior of a believer. Yet we don't often acknowledge this truth
and bury our heads in the sand hoping it will all go away on its
own. Somehow we have bought into the notion that if we don't talk
about it everything will be fine. If we don't address demons they
won't bother us. C.S. Lewis, a famous Christian writer, warned of
two dangers in his book, *The Screwtape Letters*: (1) giving too

much attention and credence to the devil or (2) ignoring him, pretending he isn't there.[1]

When I was a youngster I enjoyed the Roadrunner cartoon. Wile E. Coyote spared no expense to catch his prey, the Roadrunner, always without success. Being fooled by the Roadrunner, he would run off a mountain path, become stranded in midair over the menacing canyon below. As long as he didn't look down, he didn't fall. Suspended there for a few precarious moments, his eyes would peer below his floating feet, and, looking down, he would fall to the bottom in a puff of dirt. When it comes to dealing the spiritual bondages in our lives, we are like Wile E. Coyote. We think that if

> Deliverance for the lost
> brings them to Christ,
> and for the believer,
> it is a tool of sanctification.

we don't look down, we won't fall. If we just ignore the fact that we are bound by rejection or enslaved by a habit, it will go away. If we just keep going, we won't fall and be crushed. We have become great pretenders.

To qualify this I need to explain that not everyone who feels rejection needs deliverance. Not everyone who gets angry is demonically bound. There are some, however, who cannot pray away their rejection or anger. There are many living with the spirit of self-hatred who have read the Word, counseled with godly people, confessed their sin, forced a smile, praised the Lord—and it still won't go away. They need deliverance. The good news is, that is why Jesus came. That is why He sent the Holy Spirit. That is why He has given us His Word and His authority.

THE ANGRY ELDER

Daniel was an elder in his church. He was a godly man who loved his wife, had an orderly home, loved the Word of God, prayed and fasted, served earnestly, and was respected by all who knew him. Daniel had a problem, though. When working with his pastor, Daniel would occasionally have outbursts of anger, evidenced by curt remarks and controlling behavior. It was not uncommon to hear him say, "It's just the way I am," or "I've been this way all my life," or that he just had a more assertive personality. Like a pressure-cooker, he would eventually come to a full boil with steam billowing out of his ears. He made every attempt to keep his rage under control, but to no avail. The relationship with his pastor kept declining; something would have to give soon.

About this time, Daniel heard about Cleansing Stream Ministries. His pastor had also heard of the ministry and felt it could be trusted as it was under the covering of The Church On The Way, where Dr. Jack Hayford served. Daniel lead a small group at the church in the Cleansing Stream Seminar (the seminar that prepares the participant to receive deliverance). They then attended a Regional Retreat that was held in Southern California. While Daniel and his wife were at the Retreat, something wonderful happened. An opportunity came for those who had ongoing trouble with a spirit of anger. He was prayed for, and God delivered him; yet, he knew there was something else feeding his anger.

Later, the subject of abandonment came up. Daniel had never known his father. Conceived out of wedlock, he grew up with shame and a deep sense of being forsaken. As a young man his response to these feelings was to become angry and aggressive.

Before coming to the Lord, he had been a drug dealer. At one time he even contemplated suicide. This was Daniel's background. Coming to Christ gave him a new beginning. He loved the Lord with all his heart, yet he still embraced the lie that those in authority cannot be trusted. He thought, however subconsciously, that the only way to keep things from going wrong was to be controlling. He had not forgiven his father for abandoning him. He had brought this "extra baggage" into his Christian walk. Daniel had learned how to cope with his problem—he built a cistern to accommodate his life as it was—but it was broken and couldn't contain what he put into it. He needed living water, but didn't know how to obtain it in this area of his life. Like all of us, we are a work in progress. We are being sanctified. At the Retreat, Daniel received prayer and he was delivered from the spirit of abandonment. The source of his anger was no longer there. Abandonment could no longer feed anger. The anger was then easily removed.

Daniel and his wife returned home and attended church the following Sunday. They asked the pastor if they could speak with him in one of the Sunday School rooms following the service. The pastor was somewhat concerned but met them in the room. Daniel and his wife had prepared a bowl of water and a hand towel. With tears they asked the pastor to forgive them for their hurtful attitude, and asked if they could wash his feet. The pastor was humbled, and together they thanked the Lord and cried tears of joy. Not long after, the entire church, along with the pastor went through The Cleansing Stream Seminar. It brought health and vitality to their church.

There is a Source for the Church; there is a Redeemer, a Deliverer—Jesus Christ. He has come to set captives free. He has come to heal the brokenhearted and bind up their wounds.

Allowing Him to bring His freedom to our lives means that we first must pull our heads out of the sand and realize that our own efforts have resulted in useless, holey buckets. We need to turn to the Lord in repentance and welcome His delivering power to set us free from every bondage.

THE SICKENING MEMORY

Every year our ministry receives hundreds of testimonies from ordinary people like Daniel who have experienced an extraordinary touch from God. One such story came from a thirty-year-old woman whom I'll call Jennifer. She grew up in what appeared to be a loving family. But there was a dark secret that overshadowed this seemingly normal home. Jennifer had an uncle whom I'll call Mike. Mike would often baby-sit for Jennifer and repeatedly raped her from the time she was seven until the age of fourteen when her family moved away.

Later on, Jennifer became a Christian, married, and became a member of a wonderful church. She grew in the Lord, yet there was a persistent heaviness over her life. She did everything she could to experience the joy others seemed to have in Christ. She worshiped God with all her heart, but it felt as if a large rock was tied to it. Emotionally, she was frozen, completely bound up. But Jennifer had learned how to cope. She could smile with the best of them, so no one realized what deep wounds she carried in her soul. However, if her uncle's name came up she would become violently sick, even to the point of throwing up. *It's just the way I am—I just need to learn to live with it*, she thought.

Her church began The Cleansing Stream Seminar and she joined in, and she attended the Regional Retreat in her area. During the ministry time we addressed the area of abuse. Jennifer came forward not knowing what to expect. Would she make a fool of herself? Would she scream or become sick? As she shared in a letter sent to our office following the Retreat, nothing spectacular happened. She did experience a genuine peace, but nothing earth-shaking.

Two weeks later her sister called on the phone and expressed a desire to have a family reunion. During the conversation several names were discussed for the purpose of inviting them to attend. Mike, her uncle, was mentioned as one who should be invited. They spoke at some length about Mike attending. It was agreed that he

When we accommodate
strongholds in our lives,
we build broken cisterns
that hold no water.

should come. Jennifer's sister knew nothing of his abusiveness to Jennifer when she was young. Jennifer was struck with a realization following the phone call with her sister! The poison of abuse that had so wrecked her life was gone! She still had the memories, but the sickening weight of sadness and lifelessness had been removed. She was free. She felt clean and whole. The sun was brighter, the air cleaner, and her heart renewed. She had been delivered.

Both illustrations depict normal people in the church. They were not like the demoniac mentioned in Mark 5. They weren't bound in chains, howling at the moon. These were everyday people, just like the ones who sit next to us every week at church. Beneath the layer of sociability, there is often fear, anger, depression, loneliness, rejection, or hatred. Let's not ignore it. The truth will set us free. The Holy-Spirit-inspired Word of God renews our minds, and we can know the truth. Truth received, however, must become truth applied. If there is a failure to embrace deliverance as a lifestyle within the Church, captives will remain imprisoned, and broken hearts will remain shattered. Is it any wonder that so many churches experience splits and divisions? Unresolved issues bring destruction not only to ourselves but also to those around us. Galatians 5:15 says: *"If you keep on biting and devouring each other, watch out or you will be destroyed by each other"* (NIV).

Once truth is revealed there may still remain a battle, just as the Israelites did in taking hold of their Promised Land. But when we take the sword of the Spirit, which is the Word of God, and put our faith in what the Lord has promised, we can fight our way to freedom. James 4:7 tells us: *"Therefore submit to God. Resist the devil and he will flee from you."* It is possible to have a church that moves in balanced, biblical, no-nonsense deliverance. Thousands are doing it. The benefits are wonderful, as we'll see more clearly in chapters to follow.

Note
1. C. S. Lewis, *The Screwtape Letters*, (New York, NY: MacMillian Publishing Company, 1961), p. 3.

Chapter Three

SOMETHING WONDERFUL IS ABOUT TO HAPPEN

*So he made a whip out of cords, and drove all
from the temple area, both sheep and cattle; he
scattered the coins of the moneychangers and
overturned their tables. To those who sold doves
he said, "Get these out of here! How dare you
turn my Father's house into a market!"*
JOHN 2:15-16 (NIV)

I can only imagine what it must have been like to see Jesus drive
out the moneychangers. What an opposite scene to the one where
He takes the little children in His arms and blesses them. Does this
account demonstrate any less love? I don't think so. It was out of
His desire to see His Father's house restored to purity that Jesus
passionately cleansed the temple that day. And His actions then
speak volumes today about how passionate He is to see us become
the pure and holy places of God's presence that He designed us to

be. The Bible says that our physical bodies are the temple of the
Holy Spirit (see 1 Corinthians 6:17). God no longer dwells in
buildings built by human hands, but He lives in His people—they
are His residence. As such, it might be the case that Jesus wants
to overturn some of our tables too.

Just like the event described in John 2, our adversary, Satan,
wants to set up shop in our lives. He wants to bring in his impish
moneychangers to take advantage of us and to turn our thoughts
away from the Lord. He wants to torment us, steal from us, and
render us useless for the advancement of God's Kingdom. The
temple in Jesus' day had become noisy, smelly, distractive, and
coercive. A mockery had been made of the required sacrifices.
Blemished animals were sold at premium prices. It was a grievous sight. Those who should have been ready to lead people into
honest worship were instead caught up in the profitability of the
day.

God's people came into the temple to get their lives right
with God, but were met by ruthless leaders who took advantage
of them and stole away the possibility of worshiping in Spirit and

God's wrath is not
against those in bondage,
but against those
who are holding them there.

in truth. The Lord's anger was aroused, not against those who
sought to worship Him, but against those who occupied a place
where they did not belong. This is a perfect picture of the be-

liever in Jesus Christ whose "temple" is cluttered with unclean spirits whose aim it is to mock God and ruin lives. Please note that
Jesus did not drive out those seeking to worship. He raised His
hands and voice against the trespassers and merchandisers.

You may have heard the expression, "God hates the sin, but
loves the sinner." This is true. God wants to cleanse us, His temple.

> ### Deliverance is
> ### the means by which God
> ### brings us to a place
> ### of Christ-centeredness.

He comes to us with His Word and, if necessary, a stinging lash to
drive out the enemy. It is His love that seeks to purge us from the
demonic. Only then are we ready to honor and serve Him. Only
then do we begin to truly understand and experience the purpose
for which we were created. Until we are cleansed, we are over-
whelmed by the distracting noises of our wounds and weaknesses.
Our sin drowns out the calling of God upon our lives. We live self-
centered, preoccupied with our lives—both our limitations and our
habits. It is only when those impish moneychangers who seek to
make merchandise of us are kicked out, that we can become Christ-
centered. As the distractions in our souls are driven out by God's
power, we can more fully yield to His will for our lives. Our focus
is no longer upon our needs and hurts but is placed on the One who
has met us in our weakness and loved us to freedom and wholeness.

WE HAVE A CALL TO DELIVER

"And he who had died came out bound hand and foot with grave-clothes, and his face was wrapped with a cloth. Jesus said to them, 'Loose him, and let him go.'" (John 11:44).

At the command of Jesus, Lazarus was raised from the dead. He walked out of a grave and into a new life. Yet he was encumbered with old graveclothes. Though he was reborn, there needed to be a shedding of the past. Those graveclothes that were meant to hold him in a silent, eternal sleep had to come off so that he could enjoy the new life Jesus had granted him. It is interesting to note that Jesus did not personally unwrap His friend Lazarus. Instead He said to His disciples, "Loose him, and let him go." He entrusts into the hands of others the care of those held captive. Our task is simple. We must loose the wrappings that bind us and others to that which has no life. Jesus makes it clear that we are indeed *"our brother's keeper"* (Genesis 4:9). Wherever human bondage is found, we are challenged to participate in removing its "grave-clothes" so that the life of Christ might be made manifest.

WORLDWIDE CLEANSING

Cleansing Stream Ministry continues to expand at an amazing rate. In a few short years, we have partnered with several thousand churches in the United States and around the world. At the writing of this book, we are sending teams into over twenty nations— partnering with pastors to assist them in the discipleship of those in their congregations in the ministry of deliverance. Entire cities are mobilized, and churches are working together to see the Gospel opened up to their city.

This expansion made me realize that God's hand is upon what we are doing. "Why," I asked Him, "are you doing this now? Why is it that all around the world pastors are willing to open up to the ministry of deliverance?" I had always thought that the Lord was preparing a bride without spot or wrinkle in preparation for His coming again. While this is true, He provided me with a very simple insight. He impressed me with this thought: People in the world are broken, wounded, and lost apart from Christ. If they are won to Jesus and come into a church that is also broken and wounded, how can we disciple them? The truth is that many in the Church are in just such a condition. God wants to cleanse His Church. I believe that before the return of Christ, there will be a worldwide revival—one last ingathering. The Church must be prepared to minister the love of Jesus by proclaiming liberty to the captives. I am now motivated more than ever to fulfill His calling upon us.

DELIVERANCE IN EVANGELISM

A few years ago, I was in Portland overseeing a Regional Retreat. About two thousand people had gathered from about sixty different churches to receive ministry in the areas of deliverance and

Deliverance is
a tool of evangelism.

healing. It was an awesome time. The Lord came in great power and love. There was tremendous joy as we all experienced the loving hand of God to heal wounded hearts and cleanse lives.

We began Friday night and ended Saturday around six o'clock. I was on the platform ready to close in prayer when the Lord spoke to my heart, "Give an invitation to receive Christ." I hesitated, "Are You sure You want me to do this? After all, the people here have just gone through several months of preparation in the Seminar and now this Retreat. They've been healed and delivered. Surely they couldn't come through all this and not know You," I argued. I can imagine the people wondering what I was doing just standing there—not realizing that I was debating with the Lord. Of course, I presented the gospel, taking no more than five minutes to explain His gift of salvation. About seventy people received the Lord that night.

After the Retreat, I studied all the places in the New Testament where people fell down and worshiped Jesus. To my surprise, most of these acts of worship were preceded by someone's healing or deliverance. In response to seeing God's love reach into someone's life with tender healing and restoration, they then bowed down and worshiped Him. Psalm 34:8 invites: *"Oh, taste and see that the LORD is good; blessed is the man who trusts in Him."* Since that Retreat I have seen scores of people come to the Lord as a result of experiencing His delivering power. They gladly receive the One who loved them enough to meet them at their point of need.

Chapter Four

ESSENTIALS
FOR SUCCESS

*For the secret power of lawlessness is
already at work; but the one who now holds
it back will continue to do so till he is
taken out of the way.*

2 THESSALONIANS 2:7 (NIV)

The spirit of lawlessness is already active in this world. It
is the Holy Spirit who is holding back the tide of evil
until it is time for it to be removed. Ministry led by the Holy
Spirit is essential if we are going to effectively dislodge the
kingdom of darkness. Over time we have learned some key
lessons that will ensure successful deliverance ministry. These
lessons have been learned through much prayer and study, seeking God's wisdom, and living in His grace. I pray that every
effort will be made to incorporate these principles into the life
of your church.

PASTORAL COVERING

Whenever our ministry conducts a Regional Retreat we always invite pastors in the area to come without charge to view or participate in all that we do. The primary reason for this is because of our firm belief that deliverance ministry in the local church requires pastoral covering. In fact, we believe so strongly in this that we only release the second of our seminars, The Cleansing Stream Discipleship Seminar (the Seminar that prepares the participants to minister deliverance), for use within the local church with the pastor's full approval and involvement. Over the years we have earned the trust of pastors because of that fact.

The ministry of deliverance cannot be placed in the hands of those who seek to build their own little kingdoms. For all the great benefits that come from legitimate deliverance, it can also attract the weird and the wacky. This has often given deliverance a bad reputation. The pastor must heed the Scripture admonition, *"Know those who minister among you"* (1 Thessalonians 5:12, KJV). After all, a primary role of a pastor is to protect the flock of God. Wolves would like to come in and decimate the sheep. Pastors must guard them from potential hazard—either in word or in deed.

Pastors also bring encouragement and comfort to people as they go through deliverance. It can be a scary thing to face personal weakness. Our frailty is much more apparent than we'd like to think. It is comforting to have the encouraging words of a pastor when we acknowledge the points of sin through which the enemy has established a foothold in our life. But God gave us pastoral leadership to walk us through those difficult times.

The shepherd-king David wrote: *"Even though I walk through the valley of the shadow of death, I will fear no evil, for you are with me; your rod and your staff, they comfort me"* (Psalm 23:4,

NIV). The shepherd's rod and staff were for the purpose of protecting, guiding, rescuing, and numbering the sheep. It is a comfort to know that those in spiritual authority over you care about you enough to guard and guide you.

I have a personal passion to bless pastors. Cleansing Stream Ministries' mission statement and much of our literature uses the phrase, "partnering with pastors around the world." Pastoral covering within the local church is very important as seen in the following letter relayed to me by a pastor-friend:

"I believed strongly in the ministry of deliverance; in fact, it had been a tool God used to bless my own life. Now through The Cleansing Stream Seminar, I had an opportunity to see my congre-

> Within the local church
> the watchful eye of the pastor
> is an essential deterrent
> to wolfish activity.

gation experience freedom the way that I had. After a year of wonderful breakthroughs and growth through the use of that Seminar, I decided to utilize The Cleansing Stream Discipleship Seminar for a select group of leaders and potential leaders within the church. It grew and developed wonderfully. People were being ministered to and strongholds were being broken. I had great trust in the couple that led the group, though I warned them to be aware of any pride that might enter in. My words were prophetic. I had become uninvolved in the day-to-day deliverance activities, and things had gone amiss. I had reason to suspect pride developing within the leader and his wife and requested to meet with them. I shared my concern in a loving way, but it was met with hurt and indignity. Within a week, they led a virtual revolt among the leadership team. There was resentment among some due to my renewed involvement in what they were doing, and they had been poisoned with the thought that I was jealous of the other couple and wanted to get rid of them. Elitism had shown its ugly face. It nearly ruined this vital ministry. I learned from this costly mistake that I must stay involved."

When evaluating a deliverance ministry team, there are certain red flags to watch for. Their presence can be a sign that trouble is brewing:

1. Leaders developing a sense of "personal ownership" of the ministry that is dominating or controlling;
2. A pastor's questions and inquiries are met with resentment or viewed as a sign of mistrust on the leader's part;
3. Indications that the ministry team views themselves as having special insight and power that others don't have;
4. Team members looking down upon those who have not availed themselves yet of the ministry;
5. Team leaders or members becoming involved with peripheral and "mysterious" theology such as extended conversations with demons and/or an infatuation with angels;
6. Any signs of lack of accountability;
7. Any diminishing of all focus and all glory being put on Jesus and the triumph of His Cross and resurrection.

It might seem strange that I would emphasize these dangers while trying to promote deliverance. I believe strongly in deliverance and do not want to see the very things continued that have given it a bad name.

Of course there are numerous other occasions where proven, trusted, God-fearing elders and leaders have been given the responsibility of a deliverance ministry, and the ministry has flourished. Humility of heart toward God and others, and walking in the fear of the Lord are the ultimate keys to success...to any ministry.

SOUND TEACHING

This is very important. Many churches have been shipwrecked on the rocks of unsound doctrine. How tantalizing the dark and hidden things can be. It is so easy for the minister of deliverance to become captivated with the spirit of Gnosticism. In Colossians 1:9-14, Paul was exposing this wicked heresy in the church of Colossae. Gnostics valued the gathering and accumulation of knowledge. But knowledge in itself is empty; what is really important is a transformed life. Paul wanted two things for the Colossian church: that they would be filled with the knowledge of

Effective deliverance
is the result of being
grounded in
God's Word and ways.

God's will through all spiritual wisdom and understanding, and that they would bear fruit in every good work, growing in the knowledge of God (see vv. 9-11). Having a multitude of knowledge without it becoming profitable for living the Christian walk is futile. The true knowledge of God is not something to be kept secret, reserved only for the elite few. It is meant to be available for everyone.

I have sought to keep our ministry directed on the evidence of Scripture. While I am intrigued with various aspects of deliverance and have wondered about the truth of certain matters, I have avoided introducing them without clear biblical precedent.

DISCIPLESHIP TRAINING

I was being interviewed by a Christian publication when the writer asked, "Cleansing Stream is a deliverance ministry, right?" Although I had not anticipated my response, I said, "No, it's not. It is a discipleship ministry. We disciple people in the ministry of deliverance." There is a big difference. My personal vision is that every local church in the world would be equipped to minister deliverance, and that it would become a natural part of the fabric of the Church. Our theme Scripture is: *"And the things that you have heard from me among many witnesses, commit these to faithful men who will be able to teach others also"* (2 Timothy 2:2).

From this verse, it seems that God thinks in terms of at least four generations: *"Things you have heard from me"* (1st generation), *"among many witnesses"* (2nd generation), *"commit these to faithful men"* (3rd generation), *"who will be able to teach others"* (4th generation). If this principle were not true, you and I would never have known about Jesus Christ. It is God's way to perpetuate truth. I am a father of three children. I have seen each of our children come to Christ. But if that is as far as it goes, my discipleship will have been a failure. Only when they pass the gospel on to their children who will in turn pass it on, will I have been successful. This ministry, if it is to become a part of the garment of the

Church, must have discipleship built into it. If you do anything other than this, deliverance is doomed to become a short-lived program—and nothing more.

May I ask you something? Do you consider worship in your church a program—or is it a lifestyle? I hope you would answer, "lifestyle." Deliverance is meant to be no less. In a later chapter I'll go into detail as to how discipleship training in deliverance can also become an effective, leadership-building tool.

ACCOUNTABILITY

"And the evil spirit answered and said, 'Jesus I know, and Paul I know; but who are you?'" (Acts 19:15).

Demons understand authority. Without accountability there is no authority. Accountability empowers authority by establishing unity. Our authority comes from the Father through Jesus Christ. Our accountability is to the Holy Spirit in obedience to God's Word. And our unity with one another is through the blood of Jesus. This threefold cord is not easily broken (see Ecclesiastes 4:12).

Within the local church, all must be accountable to pastoral leadership. Apart from that, chaos ensues. We maintain this standard. Those who would minister in deliverance in the local church must have their pastor's approval before entering into The Cleansing Stream Discipleship Seminar. They must have their pastor's signature if they are to register and serve at one of our Retreats. Once in this Seminar, they are not allowed to minister deliverance within the church on their own without their team, or without the pastor's approval. If any of these rules are violated, we advise pastors to remove them from service for a period of time.

There is another aspect of accountability that deserves some attention. The Bible says that we see in part and hear in part. No one has a corner on the truth. When ministering deliverance to someone, it is always advisable to have two or more people in attendance. While one is ministering, the others are listening to the Lord and/or doing warfare. Words of knowledge and wisdom can be offered if we are willing to submit to one another for the benefit of the one being prayed for. Accountability means that I acknowledge the benefit others can bring into any given situation, and the correction that can come to keep me on course. Accountability edifies the Body of Christ.

A SAFE ENVIRONMENT

"Love suffers long and is kind; love does not envy; love does not parade itself, is not puffed up; does not behave rudely, does not seek its own, is not provoked, thinks no evil; does not rejoice in iniquity, but rejoices in the truth; bears all things, believes all things, hopes all things, endures all things" (1 Corinthians 13:4-7).

It takes courage to confess and renounce sins. It takes courage to submit to someone who will lay hands on you for the purpose of casting out unclean spirits. If a safe place is not provided, deliverance will falter. A safe place requires the following components:

1. **Confidentiality is strongly guarded.** An appointed prayer team was ministering to Bill. This team was being trained in The Cleansing Stream Discipleship Seminar. Bill shared an area of weakness over which he had struggled for years. God's hand moved in a powerful way, and Bill experienced a newfound freedom. The next morning at church, Alex, who was

one of those who had prayed the previous evening in the group, exclaimed to Bill, "Wow, Bill. God really delivered you as we prayed last night, didn't He?" Bill was humiliated in front of his friends. He felt exposed and betrayed. As a result, Alex was removed from the Seminar as a disciplinary measure.

2. **The people ministering are trustworthy and mature.** It is vitally important that only those chosen by the pastor be permitted to take part in deliverance training (like The Cleansing Stream Discipleship Seminar), and then lay hands on others as ministers. There were people in my church that I knew were not ready to minister deliverance—even though they seemed to have qualified in every other respect. I knew my flock. Some of them needed to mature.

3. **Ministers are not shocked by revelations of sinful behavior.** Shame plays a huge role when it comes to deliverance. For many, shame has kept them from seeking any help. They are petrified that someone might discover the truth of what they have done or what has been done to them. One careless remark like, "Wow, you've really lived some life!" would be all it takes to send that person running.

4. **People are not showcased for others to see.** It can be a heady thing to come up against the demonic and prevail. It is exciting to know that God can use you, and that He has truly given us authority over the ruler of this world. If we are not careful, we can allow pride to enter and parade the hurts and pains of others before a watching, admiring crowd. Who gets the glory?

Who looks so good? Whose ego gets puffed up? And who is humiliated before others? Often Jesus protected against this by leading the person receiving ministry away from the crowd (see Mark 7:33 and 8:23). This trap must be avoided at all costs.

5. **Love and grace are demonstrated.** When forcefully addressing demons, we must never forget that there is a real person before us that deserves our love and kindness. I think of Jesus' compassion as He would speak with and touch lepers, the outcast of society (see Mark 1:40-42).

I am fully persuaded that the power behind deliverance is the love of God. It is the overcoming force for which the armies of hell have no counter-defense.

There was a woman whose husband was an alcoholic. She had endured thirty years of pain, living with a man who had squandered their money and filled their home with fear, anger, blame, and rejection. He was writhing on the floor beside her as other men were ministering deliverance. His face was contorted with overwhelming darkness. But she felt nothing—no love, no mercy—nothing. The flame of affection had been snuffed out long ago.

But God showed up, and the love of God swept over her. She looked at this pathetic figure of a man who was her husband, and grace and love poured in. She fell at his side, brushed aside one of the men who was ministering, placed her arms around her husband with her face next to his and said, "I love you. I love you. I love you!" Suddenly he went limp, his expression brightened—the demons left him. Her husband was set free. Love had conquered. There is no more powerful force in the universe than God's love. As best we can we must look at others with the compassion of Christ.

PREPARATION OF THE INDIVIDUAL

As a pastor there were many times that I prayed for people who needed deliverance. But I was bothered by how temporal their freedom seemed. More often than not, they would be back the next week needing prayer for the same thing.

In a later chapter I'll share in more detail what we have found to be essential truths and disciplines that need to be understood and embraced which will enable a person to obtain and maintain their deliverance, but I've included them briefly here. To main-

Until the mind is transformed—until there comes a revelation of what keeps opening the door to demonic control—the person is doomed to repeat their ensnared condition.

tain the deliverance God brings, we must make the following commitments:

1. Learn to walk in the Spirit.
2. Commit and consecrate everything in our lives to God.

3. Speak words of life rather than be ensnared with un-godly speech.

4. Understand God's plan and ways to cleanse us.

This is why The Cleansing Stream Seminar includes those elements to prepare the participant to receive and maintain their deliverance.

MINISTRY TO THE INDIVIDUAL

We must move away from strict head knowledge. It is possible to have a head full of truth and knowledge and never experience the freedom it speaks of. After the first four sessions of The Cleansing Stream Seminar there is a Regional Retreat (with a follow-up session several weeks after that). The church group taking the Seminar, along with other churches in their area, all meet together for a gathering lasting Friday night and all day Saturday. It is during this Retreat that trained Christians (those participating in The Cleansing Stream Discipleship Seminar in their church and released by their pastor) minister deliverance. Ministry covers a variety of areas where demonic bondage is often rooted. Great miracles and tremendous testimonies are birthed during this time. Bondage that had accompanied people for years falls away. These occasions explode with joy.

FOLLOW-THROUGH
WITH THE INDIVIDUAL

"If your right eye causes you to sin, pluck it out and cast it from you; for it is more profitable for you that one of your members perish, than for your whole body to be cast into hell. And if your right hand causes you to sin, cut it off and cast it from you; for it is

more profitable for you that one of your members perish, than for your whole body to be cast into hell" (Matthew 5:29-30).

Once people receive freedom, they must then maintain it. James 4:7 tells us: *"Therefore submit to God. Resist the devil and he will flee from you."* A huge part of maintaining deliverance is ongoing submission to God and purposeful distancing from those areas where bondage occurred. The implication of this Scripture is clear. We should do whatever it takes to rid ourselves of those things that serve as a continuous pull toward our previously ensnared condition.

Unless we change our habit patterns, we are bound to repeat our failures. This requires discipline and accountability. We devised an effective session that follows the Retreat to help people continue the work God began in their lives. A complete explanation will be given in chapter nine, but, in essence, it is simply getting people connected with others who will hold them accountable for their choices, offering encouragement and also correction. We need each other to enjoy God's liberty in its fullness. Having people we can rely upon in this regard is an imperative part of continuing to walk in freedom.

Chapter Five

RECIPES
FOR DISASTER

For everything in the world—the cravings of
sinful man, the lust of his eyes and the boasting
of what he has and does—comes not from the
Father but from the world.
1 JOHN 2:16 (NIV)

Just as sure as there are keys to successful deliverance ministry, there are also red flags that can signal its failure. As I looked over the various points to be covered in this chapter, I realized that they all have their roots in pride. This is really no surprise, though. Pride has been the root of sin since the beginning. It was pride that brought about the downfall of Lucifer (who is now known as Satan), and it is no wonder that those who would seek to oppose him would be most vulnerable to this primary sin. Casting out demons can be a heady thing. Those who minister in the area of deliverance can become enthralled by their accomplishments—dazzled by the outcome of their ministry. They can begin to see themselves as being superior and better gifted than others. These, and other foibles, can lead to downfall, and become a recipe for disaster.

CAUGHT IN HIS OWN TRAP!

Pride is the underlying reason many deliverance ministers stumble into sin and failure. The feeling of superiority, of "having it all together," causes them to disconnect from others who are meant to speak into their lives with advice and even correction. Their pride blinds them to truth and opens the door for Satan to drag them down the very path they are seeking to lead others away from. As a minister, this is a vital principle to consider. Pride makes it easy to get caught in the very trap from which you're helping someone else escape. I realize that this may sound odd— but it's true, and it needs to be said. Consider the following passage:

"Now Harbonah, one of the eunuchs, said to the king, 'Look! The gallows, fifty cubits high, which Haman made for Mordecai, who spoke good on the king's behalf, is standing at the house of Haman.' Then the king said, 'Hang him on it!' So they hanged Haman on the gallows that he had prepared for Mordecai. Then the king's wrath subsided" (Esther 7:9-10).

We read this passage and love the irony of it: Haman is hanged on his own gallows. What justice! Woven throughout this narrative, the unseen hand of God is aptly working out His purpose. Haman sought revenge on Mordecai, scheming to kill him by hanging him upon the gallows. The gallows he had built were high enough so everyone would see Mordecai's humiliation and death. Instead, when all was said and done, Haman's feet dangled in the air while Mordecai enjoyed a position of favor and esteem in the king's court. What happened? Haman's own plan was used against him. Blinded by pride, he was caught in his own trap!

This principle is seen in other portions of Scripture as well. Psalm 37 declares that *"their swords will pierce their own heart"* and *"his trouble shall return upon his own head, and his violent dealing shall come down on his own crown"* (vv. 14-16, NIV). When great adversity is met with courageous intercession, the Lord will redeem every trial, confound the enemy, and deliver His people from bondage. However, when great adversity is met with smugly spouted declarations of self-sufficiency, destruction is right around the corner. And this is the point I want to impress upon anyone who seeks to lead others to freedom in Christ—be watchful of your own life. Stay submitted to God and accountable to those in authority over you.

THE ZEALOUS COLLEGE STUDENT

A young college student came to my office to share with me a cause for which he wanted to fight. He was appalled by pornography, and wanted to join an antipornography national campaign. The cause was good and righteous, but the young man was immature. I shared with him my concern that he was not ready to deal with the intense spiritual warfare that accompanies this type of bondage. At the very least, I felt he needed to have a mature adult Christian join with him, one to whom he would be accountable. He wouldn't wait to do these things and went headlong into the fight. I asked him to keep me posted. Two months later he asked for an appointment. His voice said it all. He came to the office a broken young man. In his zeal he ran ahead of God's plan and fell into the very sin he was opposing. Pride had brought him down. The good news is that over time he was restored—but it was a costly lesson.

Having said that, let's look at other areas of potential downfall so that you can be aware of the enemy's plans and avoid them:

RECIPE FOR DISASTER #1:
ONLY THE GIFTED CAN MINISTER DELIVERANCE

One of the great joys for me is to see men and women who have been timid or shy all their lives speak with authority and cast out demons. Hazel, now sixty-five years old, hadn't smiled in over thirty years. At her church she went through The Cleansing Stream Seminar (to prepare to *receive* deliverance) and then attended a Retreat. Though a widower for five years, she had been severely abused by her husband for nearly 40. She rarely looked up—and never into anyone's eyes. She was crushed by the weight of false guilt, condemnation, and rejection.

But Hazel was delivered. On Saturday afternoon the breakthrough came, and she began to laugh and cry at the same time. There were tears of joy. Her friends watched in disbelief as she ran to them and hugged them, telling them how much she loved and appreciated their care for her over the years. The following year she was encouraged to enter into The Cleansing Stream Discipleship Seminar (to prepare to *minister* deliverance). The year after that she was at the Retreat praying for people and seeing them healed and set free from demons. What a change! If you had looked at her strictly on the surface, you never would have imagined she was capable of helping anyone.

Hazel's story is not uncommon. Every year countless people tell us how God has set them free. Now their greatest joy is to see God use them to help others experience the same thing. When we conduct a Regional Retreat in a city, there may be a thousand or more people there to receive deliverance and healing (after attending The Cleansing Stream Seminar in their church). In addition, approximately one hundred trained anointers (those being trained in their local church in The Cleansing Stream Discipleship Seminar) will pray for these people. A year or so earlier these same anointers were *receiving* deliverance. Many were hurting, discouraged and bound up by hell. Now, they are freer, in training, and ministering to others in power. There is nothing like it. What an amazing God we serve. Praise to His Name! You don't need to have special giftings, display a vibrant personality, or feel anointed. Deliverance isn't about those who are praying—it is about the wonderful God we serve and His ability to reach through us to others. We all have an opportunity to do the work of Jesus.

At my home church, The Church on the Way, in California, many leaders, who were once quietly obscure, have been raised up through Cleansing Stream Ministries' two Seminars. The delivering hand of God set them free to become that for which they were created. Jesus wants to—and He loves to—do miracles like this. He often uses what others write off as damaged goods. I would even say He does His best work with such people. Paul acknowledged this when he wrote to the church at Corinth. He said: *"God has chosen the foolish things of the world to put to shame the wise, and God has chosen the weak things of the world to put to shame the things which are mighty"* (1 Corinthians 1:27). There are rich supplies of people in every church who are hoping that God can use them. Don't buy into the lie that ministry is only for the "gifted." God can use anyone.

RECIPE FOR DISASTER #2:
EMBRACE THE DRAMATIC AND THEATRICAL

This area is perhaps the one thing that tears the fabric of God-ordained deliverance more than any other. I wince over some of the things I've seen and heard in the ministry of deliverance. If the

garment is to be whole—if deliverance ministry is
the Church—we must let go of the theatrical. Ho
the world and make disciples while looking like a three-ring-circus? There are times when every protocol is violated for the sake
of getting someone's attention or puffing up someone's ego. I
have declined to give specific examples in order to avoid sounding
as if I am belittling or degrading another ministry or minister. That
is not my purpose. I desire only to see deliverance be a God-fo-
cused encounter, not a show for idle curiosity. When I watch Jesus
in the Scriptures, He went to great lengths to avoid the "show."

*"Then some of the Pharisees and teachers of the law said to
him, 'Teacher, we want to see a miraculous sign from you.' He
answered, 'A wicked and adulterous generation asks for a miraculous sign! But none will be given it except the sign of the prophet
Jonah.'"* (Matthew 12:38-39 NIV).

There are deliverance ministers who make merchandise of those
coming for help. People who have been bruised and hurt in life are
often quite vulnerable, and they can be manipulated or taken advantage of. This is not the way Jesus ministered, and since we are
following His example, it should not be ours either. Many times
Jesus told the one He had healed or delivered to go back home, or
to tell no one (see Luke 5:14). In one case where He had just
healed a man's blindness, He went to him *privately* to reveal His
identity as Messiah. Jesus worked with large crowds, but He never
manipulated them. He ministered to hurt and broken people, but
never paraded them around to prove His authority. We could all
learn from this.

At Cleansing Stream Regional Retreats, we do not allow cam-
eras or tape recorders. People coming know they are in a safe
place. They know we will not make an example of them or do
anything to embarrass them. The large Retreat provides a certain

shield. They probably don't know those who will minister to them, and might never see them again. Anonymity can be very comforting.

If prayer teams (which will be explained in chapter eleven) are used within the local church, they will need to be instructed how to protect the dignity of the people for whom they pray.

RECIPE FOR DISASTER #3:
TALK WITH DEMONS

Satan is the father of lies. As deliverance ministers, we deal with lying spirits. The one thing I can really count on is that whatever they may say is not to be trusted. Demons have a habit of speaking. They like to argue, they sometimes brag, and often cry out. They want to distract you from your purpose—at the very least they want to delay you. Being prideful like their leader, they will sometimes tell the truth to brag about their hold on someone's life— even stating the incident that allowed them in. But, you can't go to the bank on it. You can't place your trust in their remarks.

Jesus' command
still stands:
"Cast out demons."

Some ministers have erected elaborate charts of demonic hierarchy on the basis of what demons have told them during a deliverance session. Of what benefit is this? It leads to a preoccupation with demons and removes the focus from God. So, don't have a talk, put on a show, torment them so others can see what great authority you have, or establish a theology of demons on the basis of your discussion. I am not advocating that there is never a time when you address a demon. Jesus did. However, it should be handled in the same manner a judge would handle a heckler in the courtroom. The heckler would be told to be quiet, then removed—quickly and forcefully if necessary.

RECIPE FOR DISASTER #4:
STEP OUTSIDE OF YOUR AUTHORITY

We must become acquainted with Scripture well enough to know exactly what authority we do and do not have. Concerning demons, I see no scriptural justification for telling them to "go to hell where they belong." As I mentioned earlier, we have authority to cast them out, not tell them where they are to go once they leave. In fact, I have witnessed demons laughing at the one ministering because of it. They exclaimed, "Don't they know? They can't send me there now!" Demons look for every legal loophole. We only delay deliverance by acting on authority we haven't been given.

Another area where deliverance ministers can misuse their authority concerns the person for whom they are praying. We have a saying with those who assist with anointing at our Retreats: "Don't counsel, don't counsel, don't counsel." We step out of our rightful authority whenever we take the place of the legitimate authority in that person's life. For example, it is not up to me to counsel a woman about her marriage if I am neither her husband nor her pastor. Likewise, if I am ministering to young people, I will not counsel them about decisions affecting their lives because I am not their parent. The deliverance session must be focused upon only one thing—seeing God set them free from demonic bondage. Unless we are granted authority by their authority, we should not interfere with people's lives beyond the prayer time. This is true whether ministering within a local church as a part of a prayer team, or at a larger retreat setting such as what is done at a Cleansing Stream Regional Retreat.

Recipe for Disaster #5:
Create Dependency upon Yourself

Biblical deliverance ministry should give people the tools they need to allow them to pursue their freedom. If in my ministering, I make it necessary for the person for whom I'm praying to need me every time they hit a bump in the road, then I have failed. Deliverance should not be relegated to those who are "experts." Knowledge needs to be passed along. If someone knows their authority in Christ, and recognizes the basic principles of spiritual warfare, they can partner with God to deliver themselves. Jesus did not come to make us a kingdom of priests and paupers, but a kingdom of priests. We have been given His Spirit and can learn from Him to wage victorious battle over any demonic harassment. Consider these insightful passages of Scripture:

- *"He has made us to be a kingdom and priests to serve his God and Father—to him be glory and power forever and ever! Amen"* (Revelation 1:6).

- *"But you have an anointing from the Holy One, and all of you know the truth"* 1 John 2:20 (NIV).

- *"As for you, the anointing you received from him remains in you, and you do not need anyone to teach you. But as his anointing teaches you about all things*

and as that anointing is real, not counterfeit—just as
it has taught you, remain in him" 1 John 2:27 (NIV).

I have seen quiet little grandmothers who have as much anointing as anyone. It is not about being loud (demons can hear quite
well). It is not about how well I know the Word (babes in Christ
have the authority to use the name of Jesus). It does not hinge on
the gifts I possess. The authority we have comes from God; it is
because of Him and who He is in us that we have the amazing—
and humbling—ability to minister to others. Deliverance is all about
His authority in us.

Think of it this way. A police officer just out of the academy
has as much clout as a seasoned sergeant when it comes to addressing someone who is violating the law.   Police are backed by

Remember,
Jesus is
the Deliverer.

their government, and they exercise their authority through the
badge they wear. If you ever want to question that authority, you
would quickly become aware of the power they wield! In the same
manner, we are backed by the kingdom of God, have received authority to ask anything in His Name, and have received power as
the Holy Spirit has come upon us. Demons understand authority. I
say all this to underscore that the youngest, most uneducated believer lacks nothing in Christ. As believers, each of us is ultimately
dependent on Jesus Christ and under the leadership of the Holy

Spirit. We must remind others of this truth so they won't look to us as their sole resource.

Recipe for Disaster #6:
Require People to Manifest in Particular Ways

We have the regurgitaters, sneezers, coughers, shakers, screamers, biters, jumpers, laughers, and whatever-elsers.   I have seen all these manifestations—and more—during deliverance prayer. I have also seen people smile because a heavy load was removed. There are some who simply have a tear move down their face. There are no specific effects, or manifestations, signaling someone's deliverance. We can neither demand nor imply—even slightly— that a physical manifestation is required to validate deliverance. In fact, if someone screams excessively, we command the spirit to be quiet—we won't let them put on a show.

Julie was screaming—a lot. The one ministering to her didn't know how to handle the distracting manifestation and was unable to address the spirit because of it. I came over to Julie and said, "Julie, look at me! You don't have to allow this thing to use you like this. You can take authority over it and tell it to be quiet. Tell it that now." Julie said, "You evil spirit, be quiet in the name of Jesus. I'm not putting up with you any longer!" Julie was then free to be ministered to. If people fall on the floor during prayer—when led to by the Holy Spirit, we get them up. The objective is not to have them manifest, but to see them set free.

At the end of the Cleansing Stream Regional Retreat, we invite those who wish, to give a testimony of what the Lord did for them. I was once asked why very little was mentioned by the participants about "demons." Is it a plus or a minus that few of our participants reference demons as they testify to having been released from demonic bondage? This caused me to closely examine our mission statement—and beyond that, the application of our mission.

I can now say that I am overjoyed that there is very little attention given to demons *at the point of testimonies.* A patient, having gone under surgery to remove a tumor, is more likely to glory in the success of the operation and the joy of being healthy than to celebrate the size of the tumor or details of the operation. Many times I hear participants in our Retreats share of their freedom from fear, their release from anger, or their joy and peace following years of torment from abuse. Rarely, if ever, do they mention the fact that just a few hours ago they were in an intense battle with the enemy as demons were being cast out. Instead, they praise Jesus the Deliverer and give Him the glory!

Part Two

THE
CLEANSING
STREAM
MODEL

Chapter Six

PREPARING THE SAINTS FOR WAR

Do you not know that in a race all the runners
run, but only one gets the prize? Run in such
a way as to get the prize. Everyone who competes in
the games goes into strict training. They do it to get a
crown that will not last; but we do it to get a crown
that will last forever.
1 CORINTHIANS 9:24-25 (NIV)

A nthony was a sophomore in college. As he ambled slowly into the church, I could see he was in great distress. Following the evening service he asked to speak with me. In my office he confessed to an addiction to pornography. At the end of our conversation he repented before God, renounced the sin, and closed the door he had opened to unclean spirits. I prayed over him, and together we took authority over every perverse spirit and cast them out of his life. He had a new countenance. The light was back in his eyes and his head no longer hung in shame. He was free—until the following week. This pattern repeated itself another time. When he asked for the third time if I would pray deliverance over him, I said, "No." A shocked look came over him. After all, I was a pastor, and pastors are supposed to do things like this. I explained, "Anthony, you're not serious about this. You want to feel better, but you don't want to change. Not until you really want to change—not until you really want to be free—will I pray this way for you again." I went on to say, "There is something we can do. If you want, we'll pray that God will bring you to a place where you truly desire to be set free."

Through this situation, God was shaping my thoughts about deliverance. It wasn't a onetime experience. Even though God's power does bring us to a specific point of freedom, we must be ready to walk in it. Deliverance is a journey of thoughtful and deliberate obedience to the Word of God.

I began to search the Scriptures to see how God restores people to wholeness, how He brings His liberty to hurting and wounded people. Because freedom is the heart of God, I knew I would find my answer in His Word—and I did!

WE MUST BE PREPARED

"I went to Jerusalem, and after staying there three days I set out during the night with a few men. I had not told anyone what my God had put in my heart to do for Jerusalem. There were no mounts with me except the one I was riding on. By night I went out through the Valley Gate toward the Jackal Well and the Dung Gate, examining the walls of Jerusalem, which had been broken down, and its gates, which had been destroyed by fire" (Nehemiah 2:11-13 NIV).

Nehemiah was a wise builder. He prayed often and thought things through carefully. After years of exile, he and the other captive Jews had been released to return to their homeland. Now was the time for restoration. He analyzed what it would take to rebuild the walls and gates of Jerusalem after their long time in captivity. If they had merely approached the walls and started working, they might have run out of materials or manpower. Nehemiah made lists, procured supplies, arranged deliveries, gathered resources, and devised a plan that brought success. They did rebuild. God did restore.

Similarly, if he had not prepared his heart to lead God's people through this challenging season, he might have succumbed to the manipulation and insincerity of the leaders of the surrounding lands. And those neighboring leaders did try! They ridiculed Nehemiah and God's people, offered them tempting compromises, promised grand appeasement, and even threatened total destruction. They tried to wear the Jews down through discouragement, bribery, and fear, but Nehemiah was prepared. He knew what God wanted, and he had God's plan to get there. His preparation had allowed God to lead him to the other side victoriously.

In the New Testament, Jesus taught of the importance of making thoughtful decisions when it comes to God's Kingdom as well. He said, *"Suppose one of you wants to build a tower. Will he not first sit down and estimate the cost to see if he has enough money to complete it? For if he lays the foundation and is not able to finish it, everyone who sees it will ridicule him, saying, 'This fellow began to build and was not able to finish.'"* (Luke 14:28-30). One of the challenges with deliverance is that sometimes people aren't prepared to receive it. As a result, they return to the very behavior that opened the door to demonic bondage. People do not take the time to ready themselves to live a new life; they don't diligently submit their lives to the

Lord and seek His grace to change their old thoughts and habits. Instead, they live the same way they always have, and sometimes find themselves trapped again in familiar bondages.

Other factors can contribute to unfortunate relapse, but not being prepared certainly is one of them. The Bible says in Psalm 119:11: *"I have hidden your word in my heart that I might not sin against you."* If we do not have the abiding Word of God in us, it

If we are to be successful
in deliverance we must
understand the value
of preparation.

becomes difficult for us to be convicted by the Holy Spirit of sin. Without His conviction, we are unable to avoid the pitfalls of the enemy.

After years of observation and study, I believe there are four primary principles of God that need to be in place in order to aid in preparing the candidate for deliverance: walking in the Spirit, committing everything to God, speaking words of life, and entering the cleansing stream. This is why The Cleansing Stream Seminar includes those truths as sessions leading up to the Retreat—in order to prepare the participant to receive and maintain their deliverance. The necessity of working through each one of these principles, implementing its truth into everyday life, cannot be understated. True deliverance comes from thoughtful preparation, and these four principles, in my experience, are the roadmap to success. Let's look at each principle individually.

FIRST:
WALK IN THE SPIRIT

Inspired by God, Paul wrote: *"I say then: Walk in the Spirit, and you shall not fulfill the lust of the flesh"* (Galatians 5:16). Many Christians have little understanding on the subject of walking in the Spirit; in fact, they are rarely aware of when they walk in the flesh. Let's begin by clarifying terms. When we use the term, "walk in the Spirit," it implies certain actions similar to physically walking:

1. There is a destination or purpose.
2. We must stay on the pathway.
3. It is a step-by-step process.
4. We must be watchful.
5. It requires balance.

Walking in the Spirit is learning to live our lives in step with the Holy Spirit, walking with purpose on His pathway, one step at a time. This requires watchfulness and balance, both of which come as we commit to being people of God's Word and infusing our souls with His will and wisdom from the Scriptures.

If we are to walk in the Spirit, it is helpful to understand how God put us together. Specifically, we need to understand the relationship of spirit, soul, and body. (My purpose here is not to do a complete teaching, but rather to explain the reasons behind what we do and why we do it. In my opinion, this chapter is crucial to understanding why God has used Cleansing Stream Ministries to bring breakthrough in people's lives.) Some would argue that understanding about spirit, soul, and body is irrelevant to casting out demons. They say it doesn't matter if the demon is joined to my spirit, operating through my soul, or attached to my body—I just need to be free. Others would say that there is not sufficient biblical evidence to distinguish the difference between spirit and soul. To be sure, there are reputable scholars that disagree on many of these issues. Acknowledging that, I will give you the reasons why I believe it is important to teach and understand the difference in order to be prepared to live out the deliverance God's power can bring to our lives.

The Bible says, *"May God himself, the God of peace, sanctify you through and through. May your whole spirit, soul and body be kept blameless at the coming of our Lord Jesus Christ"* (1 Thessalonians 5:23, NIV). Now, if this is a request of Scripture, we should heed what it is says and see this accomplished in our lives. Note the word "sanctify." It is key to our understanding of this subject.

I was training to be a branch manager of a savings and loan in Lynwood, California. I was responsible for all new accounts and was managing several account representatives. During lunch breaks, I would often share my faith in Christ. One day an account rep. confided to me that she thought there was no more hope for her. She had given her life to the Lord as a young girl but had failed God terribly, and she now felt she had lost her salvation. No matter what comfort was presented from God's Word or encouragement from God's love, she held fast to her theology of doom. Like many others, she questioned how people who truly are Christians could commit flagrant sin. She couldn't understand how she could have done the things she did if she really was saved. Understanding about spirit, soul, and body provides the answers.

SPIRIT, SOUL, AND BODY

The essence of our being is our spirit. Our spirit needs to be quickened or made alive through receiving Christ and having the Holy Spirit indwell us. As a Christian, our spirit is perfect before God.

It is the dwelling place of the Holy Spirit. Our spirit can grow as we continue to walk with God and trust in Him. And, as the dwelling place of the Holy Spirit, it is like the Holy of Holies where the presence of the Lord dwelt. My friend, the late Walter Martin, used to say, "If a demonic spirit comes to the door of your spirit, it is met by the Holy Spirit—and the Holy Spirit will not dwell in a duplex." It is here, in our spirit, where the word "justification" is realized. When we receive Christ, He justifies us in God's sight—that is, He declares us "not guilty" (see Romans 5:1) and removes

> Justification makes room
> for sanctification. Knowing I have
> His righteousness motivates
> me to be righteous.

our sins from us *"as far as the east is from the west"* (Psalm 103:12). Justification sets us on the right road and fills our heart with joy and hope, but God's work in us doesn't stop there.

The prophet Jeremiah declared, *"In His days Judah will be saved, and Israel will dwell safely; Now this is His name by which He will be called: THE LORD OUR RIGHTEOUSNESS"* (Jeremiah 23:6). In justification, the righteousness of Jesus Christ has become ours. It is not that God has erased our sins—it is as if they never existed! Then Paul adds in his letter to the Hebrews, *"Their sins and their lawless deeds I will remember no more"* (Hebrews 10:17).

Secondly, our soul is made up of our mind, emotions, and will—and here is where the battleground of temptation and torment takes place! The devil will use every resource available to him. He will attempt to reason with you so you might question God's Word. He will attempt to make you fearful or angry. He will do everything he can to wear you down, weaken your will to resist, and persuade you to make unwise choices.

Finally, we are physical beings. We live in a physical body that is subject to its own demands. Through the appetites and cravings of the body, the enemy may tempt you with addictive or violent behavior.

Let's take a closer look at how justification and sanctification work together.

A Dynamic Duo

"For by one offering He has perfected forever those who are being sanctified" (Hebrews 10:14).

This verse says so much. No longer are yearly sacrifices required to keep our hearts clean before God. Jesus Christ has come and paid the price once and for all for our sins. But look again at this verse from Hebrews. It says that He has perfected forever those who are being sanctified. How can you be perfect, yet be in the process of sanctification? This Scripture used to puzzle me because it seemed like I was hearing double-talk from God. But as I came to better understand how God put us together—spirit, soul, and body—I saw that our *spirit* is made perfect, and our *soul* is being sanctified. Our standing in Christ before God is perfect. By faith I receive eternal life (justification in my spirit) and by that same faith understand that I am a work in progress (sanctification in my soul). Second Corinthians 1:10 explains that Jesus *"delivered us from so great a death, and does deliver us; in whom we trust that He will still deliver us."* He has delivered us—this is my past, from which I can say I have been justified (spirit). He does deliver us—this is my present, in which I can say I am being sanctified (soul). He will still deliver us—this is my future in which I can say I will be glorified (body).

The Holy Spirit assures me that I am a child of God, for His Spirit (capital *S*) bears witness to my *spirit* (lower case *s*) that I am

"And do not be conformed to this world, but *be transformed by the renewing of your mind*, that you may prove what is that good and acceptable and perfect will of God."
ROMANS 12:2 (EMPHASIS ADDED)

a child of God (see Romans 8:16). While He does this, He is also transforming my *soul* into the image of His dear Son.

While we cannot understand exactly how the Holy Spirit does His amazing work of sanctification in our lives, we can rejoice that He does! *"But we all, with unveiled face, beholding as in a mirror the glory of the Lord, are being transformed into the same image from glory to glory, just as by the Spirit of the Lord"* (2 Corinthians 3:18).

Understanding about spirit, soul, and body enables us to cooperate better with the Holy Spirit as He does His work. It also encourages us when we might feel despair over our condition. We see our flaws and imperfections and are still able to accept ourselves because we know we are in process—walking in the Spirit—yet fully acceptable to the Lord. *"There is therefore now no condemnation to those who are in Christ Jesus...who do not walk according to the flesh, but according to the Spirit"* (Romans 8:1,4).

SECOND:
COMMIT EVERYTHING TO GOD

"Delight yourself also in the LORD, and He shall give you the desires of your heart. Commit your way to the LORD, trust also in Him, and He shall bring it to pass" (Psalm 37:4-5).

Now the battle really begins. Once we begin to walk in the Spirit, we quickly realize that we have a problem. Issues keep surfacing that cause us to stumble! If we have not fully consecrated our lives to the Lord, if we haven't committed everything to Him, we will discover it here. Areas where trouble may surface include possessions, relationships, financial situations, work responsibilities, or a host of others. The point is that in these areas of conflict or tension, we must understand that the answer is to surrender to the Lord. In committing everything—every part of our lives to Him—we will find that His power is able to bring about His will, which often means changing us, not the situation.

We must hold
the template of walking
in the Spirit
over everything we do.

Perhaps our marriage is not what it should be, and we are trying to fix it in our own strength. We will have to surrender our rights and commit our spouse to the Lord, seeking His will while incorporating the truths being learned as we walk in the Spirit.

Every area of our lives must come under obedience to the Lord. We must commit our family, occupation, finances, and ministry to

Him. Now we are less likely to stumble as we walk in the Spirit. However, we may discover that there are some areas that don't seem to go away quietly. This is a necessary realization for it will prepare our hearts for deliverance. Realizing that some issues cannot be dealt with apart from the intervention of God's power, allows us to receive His help. We discover the need for deliverance.

THIRD:
SPEAK WORDS OF LIFE

"Death and life are in the power of the tongue, and those who love it will eat its fruit" (Proverbs 18:21). There is little question in anyone's mind that we tend to foul ourselves up with our words. Many have overlooked the full implications of words spoken to us that we have embraced, or words we have spoken that have embraced us.

Consider this: Look around you. Do you see that chair? Where did it come from—how did it come to be? It was first a thought in someone's mind. That thought became a blueprint. Words were spoken to begin the process of manufacturing; monies were exchanged, contracts signed, production schedules formulated, marketing plans established, and commitments made for purchase by stores. The product was delivered to the store in which it was purchased and ended up in your home. All of this began with a thought, an idea; then words were spoken to put everything into action. Words have power. Our words, however, first have thoughts behind them. *"A good man out of the good treasure of his heart brings forth good; and an evil man out of the evil treasure of his heart brings forth evil. For out of the abundance of the heart his mouth speaks"* (Luke 6:45). Whose words are we listening to? The thoughts that come into our head—are they our own, or have they come from a demon? Can we recognize when a thought is the Lord's or ours? This is very important to understand because our thoughts, when acted upon, create an end result.

Jane was standing next to me in church. As we began to worship, I could faintly hear her voice—it was wonderful! At the end of the service I turned to her and remarked about her vocal gift. She said, "Oh no, I have an awful voice. I can't carry a tune in a bucket!" In amazement and curiosity I responded, "Who told you

> There is good seed and bad seed—
> producing life and death.
> It's our choice what we speak
> and what we receive.

that?" "My mother" she said. "When I was a little girl I walked into the kitchen singing and was told to shut up—that I should never sing, that I couldn't carry a tune." Jane then realized that she had embraced the words spoken to her by her mother, believing them to be true. For nearly thirty years those discouraging words had impacted her life. She asked the Lord to forgive her for believing a lie, and then she renounced and broke those words. Now she sings in churches and blesses the Body of Christ with her beautiful gift.

There are many adults who, like Jane, were told by someone in authority, "You're worthless. You're no good. You're dumb. You will never amount to anything. You're ugly. I wish you were never born!" What we say and what we chose to listen to can either bring us blessing or defeat. Words can kill, and words can give life. Jesus speaks of words as being like seed. *"Another parable He put forth to them, saying: 'The kingdom of heaven is like a man who sowed good seed in his field'"* (Matthew 13:24, NIV). The word for "seed" in the Greek is *sperma*, which by implication means offspring. In other words, our words produce life or fruit.

When the seed of a word goes into the soil of the heart, and if that heart is receptive, a crop will begin to grow. That seed, whether good or bad, will bring forth a corresponding fruit. Matthew 7:17-18 explains: *"Even so, every good tree bears good fruit, but a bad tree bears bad fruit. A good tree cannot bear bad fruit, nor can a bad tree bear good fruit."*

When we are preparing for deliverance, this subject is likely to be the toughest one to face. Many memories are stirred up and many thoughts surface—including recollections of times destructive words were embraced that have dramatically impacted our lives. But this is needful because it is a door to understanding and recognizing our need for deliverance from the bondage.

REMEMBER JABEZ?

"Now Jabez was more honorable than his brothers, and his mother called his name Jabez, saying, 'Because I bore him in pain.' And Jabez called on the God of Israel saying, 'Oh, that You would bless me indeed, and enlarge my territory, that Your hand would be with me, and that You would keep me from evil, that I may not cause pain!' So God granted him what he requested" (1 Chronicles 4:9-10).

Jabez, or *Ya 'bets* as it is literally translated, means "and he shall cause pain," cried out to God for deliverance. The exact circumstances surrounding the pain of his birth are not known. We do know that his mother exacted her pain upon her son by naming him as she did. Jabez knew that without God's intervention, he would be tempted to live out the effect of his name from birth, and would also "cause pain" (vs. 10)! His insight as to the impact previous generations can have on future ones is an example for us to follow. By confessing the truth and renouncing evil, God granted him his request and broke the effect of his name for himself and for future generations!

Whether we have spoken words that planted destruction or believed those words spoken by someone else about us, we need to come to the Lord for His delivering power. He can change the course of our lives with His Word of Truth—Jesus Christ!

FOURTH:
ENTER THE CLEANSING STREAM

"Purge me with hyssop, and I shall be clean; wash me, and I shall be whiter than snow" (Psalm 51:7). Is there anyone who doesn't praise the Lord for this truth? I can be whiter than snow—I can be purged and cleansed. Everyone needs this hope. The Bible says, *"Hope deferred makes the heart sick..."* (Proverbs 13:12, NIV). There is a dual purpose to this final principle. First, there is hope for all who find themselves polluted by their past or encumbered with the bondage of the present. Second, God has a process by which we can experience freedom from bondage.

The Scripture says, *"And do not give the devil a foothold"* (Ephesians 4:27, NIV). If we open the door to the enemy often enough, he can gain a sizeable place of influence in our lives. We have likened this bondage to fishhooks that get under your skin.

I remember as a young boy trying to cast a line from the bank of a stream. I cast my rod backward and whipped it forward only to have the hook catch my arm. It was small but caused much pain. If someone had grabbed the line attached to that hook I would have followed them anywhere.

I used to enjoy deep-sea fishing with my father. He had a little cabin cruiser that the whole family would enjoy. One day we were in some fairly choppy water. My father was down below and about to lie down since he was not feeling well. A large wave struck the boat, lifting his feet off the floor throwing him onto a small bed. Unbeknown to him, there was a large shark hook lying on top. My father's bottom met with the point of the hook—and he gave quite a shout to announce it! It was difficult to distinguish his shouting from our laughter. Painful as it was for my dad, the imagery of us removing that hook kept us laughing for several days. Thankfully, my dad had a great sense of humor.

Some hooks are larger than others, just as sometimes the place we give the enemy is more formidable than others. The point is that God doesn't want any hooks in us at all! Hooks need removal, not tolerance. Even little hooks can bring much pain and discomfort and, if left, infection. Whether we have allowed a small hook or a large one, we need to come to God's cleansing stream to receive healing and deliverance.

The cleansing process includes:

1. Seeing the truth and identifying the demonic spirit;
2. Bringing godly repentance for the actions that gave place to that demonic spirit;
3. Renouncing the door that was opened as a result of the sin;
4. Breaking the yoke of bondage and commanding the removal of all demonic presence;
5. Identifying and blessing the person with God's intentions.

These, and much more, take place at the Regional Retreats immediately following the initial four principles taught in The Cleansing Stream Seminar sessions and covered in this chapter. As I said earlier, just walking through the initial four sessions brings a measure of deliverance, because opportunity for ministry is encouraged following each teaching. During all of these sessions those preparing for deliverance will undertake additional disciplines such as Scripture reading (to hide the Word of God in their hearts), praying together (for mutual encouragement), and worshiping the Lord (to draw close to the Father). They are also supported from within the local church—people who will contact them weekly and pray that they might press on through the Seminar and not be overcome by the trials that are sure to come. The bottom line? Preparation precedes lasting deliverance. This is why the local church is a vital part of God's plan for bringing freedom to His people.

Chapter Seven

ADVANCING TO
THE RETREAT

*Therefore, leaving the discussion of the
elementary principles of Christ, let us go on
to perfection, not laying again the
foundation of repentance from dead works
and of faith toward God.*

HEBREWS 6:1

What a thrill it is to see someone set free from years of bondage! The Retreat takes place following a number of weeks of preparation and the study detailed in the previous chapter. During this extended time of preparation, people frequently discover attitudes and habits that are hindering their walk with the Lord. Such trouble spots are often because of demonic bondage, from which God intends to set them free. All of this preparation is done under the supervision of their local church conducting The Cleansing Stream Seminar, and while some deliverance comes during the time of preparation, much more will take place at the Regional Retreat itself.

For example, John was a leader in his church. He wanted with all his heart to be faithful in his spiritual responsibilities. As he was working through the workbook to reinforce the truth of walking in the Spirit, he realized that it is possible to do spiritual things in a fleshly manner. John was a manager of a large department store, and he was taught to bring in results, not excuses. He brought this same thinking into the ministry assignments given him by his pastor. John soon realized that he needed to repent of his attitude toward others whom he had manipulated to achieve his objectives. As a part of his repentance, John went to those he had pressured and manipulated and asked for their forgiveness. During this process of preparation, he was delivered from a spirit of selfish ambition (see Galatians 5:19-20). God had moved in his heart, bringing freedom and deliverance. John was that much more ready to pursue God's liberating presence at the Retreat.

PRAYER FIRST

All effective ministry begins with prayer. Though few would disagree with this statement, it is sometimes a good intention and not a real commitment. For deliverance ministry, prayer must be the backbone of every meeting, every decision, every outreach. Each year, Cleansing Stream schedules a number of Regional Retreats around the country. At each Retreat the number of people in attendance can range from four hundred to two thousand coming from churches that are conducting The Cleansing Stream Seminar. For every ten people going through the Retreat, there is normally one trained person to minister to them. What an amazing sight it is to see hundreds of trained Christians, prepared to go to battle for their brothers and sisters. These well-trained, highly devoted "anointers" come from a number of churches in the area surrounding the Retreat. All of these churches have partnered with our ministry to assist in training some of their people in effective, balanced, and biblical deliverance by conducting The Cleansing Stream Discipleship Seminar.

During each Retreat we also have up to two hundred intercessors stationed around the sanctuary offering prayer on behalf of those attending. In fact, all those who minister at one of our Regional Retreats must first have served as an intercessor. We do this for two main reasons. First, we want those being trained to minister deliverance to understand and appreciate the power of intercessory prayer. Second, it gives them an opportunity to discover that being an intercessor might be their calling rather than praying for someone coming forward for ministry. It is quite rewarding to know that all these trained people will be going back to their respective churches where they can come alongside their pastor, ready and willing to advance the kingdom of God in their city. In a later chapter, I will discuss the training process in more detail.

DOWN TO THE ROOTS

"Even so, every good tree bears good fruit, but a bad tree bears bad fruit. A good tree cannot bear bad fruit, nor can a bad tree bear good fruit. Every tree that does not bear good fruit is cut down and thrown into the fire" (Matthew 7:17-19).

"And even now the ax is laid to the root of the trees. Therefore every tree which does not bear good fruit is cut down and thrown into the fire" (Luke 3:9).

I was an associate pastor living in Texas. In our backyard stood an old ugly tree. It was close to our house so I decided to take it down before it became a hazard. Its trunk was about five inches in diameter, so I felt I could remove it myself without any difficulty.

I cut it almost flush to the ground, tying a rope around the trunk to keep it from falling on the house. It came down successfully. I chopped it up for firewood and enjoyed the benefit of its demise— until a few weeks passed. I looked outside and discovered that a twig was growing up from the stump of that old, ugly tree. *Well*, I thought, *I know how to take care of you.*

I went to the shed, brought out some pruning sheers and cut off the twig. A few weeks passed and the same thing happened again. So, out came the sheers and down came the twig. Winter came and went and nothing more happened. But then came spring. I kept my eye on where the stump was—no twigs. *Great!* I thought,

> While it is necessary to deal with sin and its effects, it is equally important to address the root causes. Otherwise, the likelihood of repetition is greatly increased.

I've finally gotten rid of you. Then, all over the yard twigs shot up with force and in great numbers. Convinced of a arboreal conspiracy, I called a friend who was not gardening-impaired. He asked, "What did you do?" I explained my adventure. He answered without hesitation, "You didn't cut out the root, did you?"

Trees are smart. I discovered that the roots of that seemingly destroyed tree still lived— and they sent forth new twigs straight up from the roots themselves! There were at least twenty throughout my back yard. We promptly proceeded to kill the root system, and that took care of my tree problem. A similar truth exists for us in our pursuit of freedom. Hebrews 12:15 warns: *"Looking care-*

fully lest anyone fall short of the grace of God; lest any root of bitterness springing up cause trouble, and by this many become defiled." In other words, if the roots are not destroyed, the behavior will continue. It may pop up in others areas, but it will find a way to grow again.

The two trees shown on the following pages reflect this truth. During the Retreat we first deal with some of the more common roots. There are spirits of rejection, for example, that if not cast out will tempt the individual into all kinds of sin. Rejection is at the root of racism. It is also at the root of suicide and murder. Unforgiveness is another common root, and so is fear, and each one produces its own kind of fruit. Beneath these roots are demonic assignments meant to perpetuate activities in keeping with those root causes. The type of sinful activity means very little to demons, as long as it alienates us from God and others.

BREAKING SOUL TIES/ "POINTS OF BONDAGE"

If we're to be delivered from deeply rooted attachments of the past, we must first understand how these roots were established. One such way is through harmful soul ties. "Soul tie" is a church term. You will not find the words "soul tie" in the Bible. You will, however, find truths concerning them in the Scriptures.

The biblical terms "knit," "joined to" and "cleave" are the most commonly used words to describe what I call a soul tie. Strong's Concordance says "knit" means "to bind up or join together." "Cleave" means "to adhere, fasten, or glue together." The phrase "joined to" means "to link or fasten together." Now this connection can be either good or bad.

Examples of good soul ties can be found in the following Scripture passages:

Death producing...

"The thief's purpose is to steal and kill and destroy..." John 10:10 (NLT)

"When you follow the desires of your sinful nature..." Galatians 5:19-21 (NLT)

Reprinted with permission from The Cleansing Stream Retreat Notebook, p. 2-2

© Cleansing Stream Ministries

Life Giving!

"...My purpose is to give life in all its fullness." John 10:10 (NLT)

"But when the Holy Spirit controls our lives..." Galatians 5:22-23 (NLT)

Reprinted with permission from The Cleansing Stream Retreat Notebook, p. 2-3
© Cleansing Stream Ministries

1. **Genesis 2:24: between a husband and wife:**
   *"Therefore a man shall leave his father and mother and be **joined** to his wife, and they shall become one flesh"* (emphasis mine).

2. **Genesis 44:30: between a parent and child:**
   *"Now therefore, when I come to your servant my father, and the lad is not with us, since his life is **bound up** in the lad's life"* (emphasis mine).

3. **First Samuel 18:1: between good friends:**
   *"Now when he had finished speaking to Saul, the soul of Jonathan was **knit** to the soul of David, and Jonathan loved him as his own soul"* (emphasis mine).

4. **Second Samuel 20:2: between the people and their leader or pastor:**
   *"So every man of Israel went up from after David, and followed Sheba the son of Bichri: but the men of Judah **clave** unto their king, from Jordan even to Jerusalem"* (KJV, emphasis mine).

5. **Deuteronomy 10:20: between us and God:**
   *"You shall fear the LORD your God; you shall serve Him, and to Him you shall **hold fast**, and take oaths in His name"* (emphasis mine).

A clear example of a bad soul tie can be found in this Scripture passage: *"And Dinah the daughter of Leah, which she bare unto Jacob, went out to see the daughters of the land. And when Shechem the son of Hamor the Hivite, prince of the country, saw her, he took* *her, and lay with her, and defiled her. And **his soul clave unto Dinah***" (Genesis 34:1-3, KJV, emphasis mine).

In this passage we find a detailed account of a forcible rape. It was not Dinah's choice to be raped. Even so, a soul tie was established. There are soul ties to everyone with whom we have had a sexual relationship. In the Retreat setting we go into great detail showing how the uncleanness of these sexual encounters are passed on to their sexual partner. We also show that there is great reason to hope and rejoice since it is a simple matter to have every one of these soul ties (whether gained by choice or against our will) broken in a matter of moments. In a loving and safe atmosphere, we

Weighed down, hindered, and plagued by the past, many Christians unnecessarily carry extra baggage of unbroken sexual soul ties into their walk with the Lord.

discretely, but forcibly, break every sexual soul tie. This is always a time of great freedom. My purpose here is not to go through the steps we take with the participants to break those ties, but rather explain the need for them to be broken. I can say this—no stone is left unturned, no root is left to resprout. When we are through, there is no doubt that every ungodly soul tie has been broken.

In speaking of this area of deliverance, I have seen couples that have been married for many years treating their spouse as if they were newly wed. Many seemingly hopeless marriages have been restored. Those who are single and have fallen into sexual sin literally jump with genuine joy as they experience the beauty of holiness in their life. Some never thought it possible that they could ever feel clean again.

FORGIVE OR FORGET THE MIRACLE

Another major root that can poison a person's life is unforgiveness. It is by far the most common reason why a person is denied freedom from demonic bondage. I have been to many countries conducting Retreats, and it the same everywhere. The common thread of bondage that weaves itself through every generation and culture is unforgiveness and bitterness. God's Word is so clear about this, and we claim to take Jesus at His Word. Yet, in the matter of forgiving others, we sometimes think that He really didn't mean it when what He said: *"But if you do not forgive men their trespasses, neither will your Father forgive your trespasses"* (Matthew 6:15). Consider the following passages from the Word of God about our need to forgive:

- *"Then Peter came to Him and said, 'Lord, how often shall my brother sin against me, and I forgive him? Up to seven times?' Jesus said to him, 'I do not say to you, up to seven times, but up to seventy times seven'"* (Matthew 18:21-22).

- *"And forgive us our sins, for we also forgive everyone who is indebted to us"* (Luke 11:4).

- *"And be kind to one another, tenderhearted, forgiving one another, just as God in Christ forgave you"* (Ephesians 4:32).

- *"Repay no one evil for evil. Have regard for good things in the sight of all men. If it is possible, as much as depends on you, live peaceably with all men. Beloved, do not avenge yourselves, but rather give place to wrath; for it is written, 'Vengeance is Mine, I will repay,' says the Lord. Therefore 'If your enemy is hungry, feed him; if he is thirsty, give him a drink; for in so doing you will heap coals of fire on his head'"* (Romans 12:17-20).

This subject is easy to teach because the Word is clear. However, it is very difficult to fully embrace because of the depth of hurt and pain people can cause. One of the most potent attacks of the enemy is offense and unforgiveness. These two ungodly weeds will attempt to strangle out the life of the Spirit. The Lord has a cure for this, just as He has for every attack of Satan, and this cure is essential if one is to receive deliverance.

Some people have been through horrendous experiences. They have been hurt, experienced deep wounds, and even been abused. At a Regional Retreat, when the leaders instruct them to forgive others, it is not justifying those who caused the hurt, nor is there any attempting to make light of those painful experiences. The truth is, though, if they do not forgive, if they are not willing to release offenses, then they will be hindered and limited in what God can do in and through them.

To illustrate this, let's look at two examples from the Bible, one where someone was offended, and another where someone refused to be. Certainly, the Lord's command alone should be sufficient for us to extend forgiveness, but the following passages provide additional motivation for us to take Him seriously.

OFFENSE TAKEN

"Jesus left there and went to his hometown, accompanied by his disciples. When the Sabbath came, he began to teach in the synagogue, and many who heard him were amazed. 'Where did this man get these things?' they asked. 'What's this wisdom that has been given him, that he even does miracles! Isn't this the carpenter? Isn't this Mary's son and the brother of James, Joseph, Judas and Simon? Aren't his sisters here with us?' **And they took offense at him.** *Jesus said to them, 'Only in his hometown, among his relatives and in his own house is a prophet without honor.'* **He could not do any miracles there,** *except lay his hands on a few sick people and heal them. And he was amazed at their lack of faith"* (Mark 6:1-6, NIV, emphasis added).

This example makes it clear that those who took offense at Jesus reflected an amazing lack of faith. This lack of faith resulted in a restriction of miracles—in effect, their refusal tied the hands of God.

OFFENSE NOT TAKEN

"Leaving that place, Jesus withdrew to the region of Tyre and Sidon. A Canaanite woman from that vicinity came to him, crying out, 'Lord, Son of David, have mercy on me! My daughter is suffering terribly from demon-possession.' Jesus did not answer a word. So his disciples came to him and urged him, 'Send her away, for she keeps crying out after us.' He answered, 'I was sent only to the lost sheep of Israel.' The woman came and knelt before him. 'Lord, help me!' she said. He replied, 'It is not right to take the children's bread and toss it to their dogs.' 'Yes, Lord,' she said, 'but even the dogs eat the crumbs that fall from their masters' table.' Then Jesus answered, 'Woman, you have great faith! Your request is granted.'

And her daughter was healed from that very hour" (Matthew 15:21-28 NIV).

This woman endured far more than most of us would be willing to. She continued to overlook the rejection of the disciples and the refusal of the Lord, because she knew that if she became offended and gave up, her daughter would never receive the healing she desperately needed. She refused to be offended, demonstrated great faith, and received her miracle.

Susan had fought fear much of her life. It had become debilitating. She rarely went outside, and when she did it was terrifying. Just two years earlier she had become a Christian. Much of

> Without stubborn refusal to engage
> in the bitter fruit of unforgiveness,
> there can never come the miraculous power of
> God to cast out demons.

her fear left her when she gave her heart to the Lord, but something continued to limit her walk with the Lord. She had difficulty trusting God and was deathly afraid of crowds. Susan attended The Cleansing Stream Seminar at her church. It was a major accomplishment for her to just to come to the Regional Retreat. It was our closing night, and Susan knew she needed to be set free. There had been little progress and she was desperate. Many of us had noticed that Susan wanted freedom but never seemed to quite get there. We addressed the area of unforgiveness with her once again. She said she couldn't think of anyone with whom she was angry. We prayed, asking God for revelation. Susan recalled an incident with her fifth grade teacher, but said it was nothing. We encouraged her to share the story. It was her turn in class to tell something about her vacation that summer. She was quite nervous, and felt she had made a fool of herself. Both the students and the teacher laughed at her. She was humiliated. The door to fear was opened. Behind that fear was a wall of anger. Very simply, and with tears of pain, she forgave the teacher and students. She asked God to forgive her for carrying that anger all these years. Anger was renounced and broken. She then repented and renounced the fear that was given subsequent entrance. In just a few short minutes, she was free! What an amazing transformation took place. The demonic bondage was broken. Susan was a changed woman.

EXERCISING OUR WILL

One of the greatest gifts God has given us is the power to choose—to exercise our will. It seems that God refuses to violate our freedom to choose. We all have heard the story of the demoniac who was filled with demons who called themselves "Legion."

"Then they came to the other side of the sea, to the country of the Gadarenes. And when He had come out of the boat, immediately there met Him out of the tombs a man with an unclean spirit" (Mark 5:1-2).

This story illustrates the power of the human will. It is obvious that the last thing these demons wished to do was meet Jesus. Yet, when Jesus got out of the boat, the demoniac was there to meet him. The will of this man was more powerful than a legion of demons.

People can be set free from demonic bondage more quickly when their will is engaged. During times of ministry, leaders en-

courage the active involvement of each participant. It is not uncommon for someone to just stand there and want others to deliver
them. People being prayed for must take an active role in their
freedom. They must repent of their sin, renounce all ties to the
enemy, and actively join in breaking the yoke of bondage. Those
who minister simply help facilitate a process that each individual
can apply.

GENERATIONAL SIN

I realize this is a touchy subject. There has been some erroneous
teaching concerning the influence that sin from previous generations can have on us leaving people to questions such as, *Because
my father sinned, does this mean that I will be held accountable?*
The answer, of course, is no. Everyone will give an account of his
or her own deeds. Second Corinthians tells us, *"For we must all
appear before the judgment seat of Christ, that each one may receive the things done in the body, according to what he has done,
whether good or bad"* (5:10).

Yet, is it possible that the implications of an ancestor's sin can
impact my life? Yes, of course. A child who is brought up in a
home with great anger will more than likely have to contend with
anger themselves throughout their life. Those who have been subject to an alcoholic parent often face the same temptation. It has
been proven that over 90 percent of sexually abused children become abusers when they reach adulthood. We see these occur-
rences in the natural, yet often fail to see the spiritual connection.
*"...Visiting the iniquity of the fathers upon the children to the third
and fourth generations of those who hate Me, but showing mercy
to thousands, to those who love Me and keep My commandments"*
(Exodus 20:5-6). Rather than a vindictive nature, this reflects God's
constant love and desire for us to avoid bondage. Deuteronomy

6:24 further says, *"And the Lord commanded us to observe all these statutes, to fear the Lord our God, **for our good always**, that He might preserve us alive, as it is this day"* (emphasis mine).

Just as God assigns angels to the heirs of salvation, Satan makes his own twisted assignments. Demons have been around for a long time. Familial spirits are those that are passed along family lines from generation to generation. I explain the influence of generational sin this way: if a previous generation fails to repent of their sin, the spirit assigned to that act will press in on the next generation. It does not mean that they will inevitably fall into the same sin. It does mean, however, that they will be more exposed to it and, as a result, more enticed to fall into the same pattern as the previous unrepentant generation. Children reared in rejection or anger are more likely to fall prey to the same bondage.

A good friend of mine named Seth pastors a church in New Zealand. He is a wonderful man of God with a wonderful family. They serve the Lord with great passion. Seth was attending one of our Retreats. At the time, we were addressing the spiritual bondage behind Freemasonry. Seth came forward for prayer, although he personally had no involvement with this organization and was unaware of any family attachment. The moment we began to minister he went through a most amazing deliverance. It totally surprised him. Some time later, his cousin took a trip to England and was at the church where his great grandfather had once been. To his great shock, a cornerstone memorial was imbedded in the church building it was dedicated to his great grandfather—a mason Grand Master!

A number of months ago I discovered that my grandfather (now deceased) was one of the highest-ranking masons in England! I was not aware of any obvious influence of this upon my life, but I knew, based on my mother's account, that my grandfather did not spiritually address his sin and error. I chose to repent and deal with any effect of this generational sin in my life and for future generations. (For an example of praying on behalf of your generations, see Nehemiah 1.) I did this not out of fear, but rather to cut off any influence of this on me, my children, and grandchildren ("to the third and fourth generation"). Instead I choose to continue

Each one of us is granted the opportunity to leave behind great spiritual blessings to our children. We also have the capacity to pass along the influence of our own bondage for future generations to contend with.

to walk in such a way that the flow of blessing is released to my generations ("to thousands") until Jesus comes.

I read a story in a newspaper some time ago about a little girl in a small Texas town. The little girl was inside the house in the kitchen while her mother was in the bedroom cleaning. Just outside the little girl could hear a dog barking. As she curiously approached the screen door she saw a little dog jumping around on the porch. From her vantage point, she didn't notice the foam on the dog's mouth—nor could she know that the dog was rabid. In all innocence she opened the door, but the dog bit her, and as a result, she contracted rabies. Doors are opened every day by God's people. Some out of curiosity, and some out of ignorance. Some of these doors are very harmful, *"My people are destroyed for lack of knowledge..."* (Hosea 4:6). As God's people, we must not only consider the effect on our lives, but also that on the lives of future generations, and choose to pass on blessing!

One of the primary purposes of the Regional Retreat is help people who have prepared themselves through The Cleansing Stream Seminar to lay an ax to the roots that have caused demonic bondage. In our own strength and wisdom, we could never over-throw the power of the enemy. But God stands with us—indeed stands in us—to bring freedom and deliverance to His people. It is His Word that sets us free. *"For the word of God is living and powerful, and sharper than any two-edged sword, piercing even to the division of soul and spirit, and of joints and marrow, and is a discerner of the thoughts and intents of the heart"* (Hebrews 4:12). Thank God that we have been given a mighty sword!

Chapter Eight

FACING
THE ENEMY

For the weapons of our warfare are not carnal but
mighty in God for pulling down strongholds, casting
down arguments and every high thing that exalts itself
against the knowledge of God, bringing every thought
into captivity to the obedience of Christ.
2 CORINTHIANS 10:4-5

DO YOU HAVE A STRONGHOLD?

Much of deliverance centers around uprooting strongholds and breaking their power over our lives. Since this is the case, it is important that we have a clear understanding of what a stronghold is. A stronghold is anything—an attitude, a thought process, a belief—that holds us in defiance of God's will or His ways, many of which are demonic in origin.

A key to this understanding can be found in 2 Corinthians 4:5. Several indicators of a spiritual bondage are listed. Paul, inspired by the Holy Spirit, tells us to fight against these—indeed, any-thing—that inhibits our understanding of the Lord or that limits us from submitting fully to His Word. Most of these things are ideas and feelings that challenge the authority of God in our lives. Con-sider the following questions:

1. Are you using physical, of-this-world means to address spiritual issues?
2. Are you continually argumentative or contrary—usu-ally on the verge of anger?
3. Are you listening and following words that contradict God's Word?
4. Is your thought-life in disarray? Is it running loose and undisciplined?
5. Are you walking in known disobedience to the Word?
6. Are you violating, neglecting or causing pain in a rela-tionship?

If one or more of these questions could be answered yes, then there is a good possibility that a stronghold exists. Strongholds don't just happen; we usually walk into them with our eyes wide open. Most of this "walking into" was motivated by pain or hurt endured—perhaps years earlier.

Brian was an angry young man. It would take very little for him to fly off the handle. His fits of screaming and yelling at those he loved made everyone miserable. When interviewed, he shared about his terrible childhood. His father was a cruel man who con-sistently tore him down with unloving and unkind words. In an attempt to hide his pain, Brian put up a wall. This went on for many years, but as he got older the pain seeped out and anger be-gan to blossom. A stronghold had been established.

If Brian's father was the instigator, and Brian the victim, why does *he* (Brian) have a stronghold? The reason is that Brian became angry and unforgiving. His thoughts got away from him, and he began to believe the lie from hell that he had a right to his anger. Bad memories reinforced his thinking, and a fortress was erected. Most all of these strongholds are poorly lit. They exist in the darkness. Satan lives in the dark. Ignorance and deception are his pathways. It takes the Word of God to shine the light of truth upon strongholds. When that revelation comes, a choice can be made: "Will I hang on to my anger, or release it?" If released, repentance will follow. If not, the walls of the stronghold grow thicker; the conscience is seared and becomes less sensitive to the voice of the Holy Spirit.

THE SEARED CONSCIENCE

"Such teachings come through hypocritical liars, whose consciences have been seared as with a hot iron" (1 Timothy 4:2, NIV).

It is possible for a believer to come to the place where his or her conscience has been seared and no longer able to hear the convicting voice of the Spirit that would bring them to repentance.

The root of the Greek word for "seared" means to cauterize and render insensitive. Before the advent of modern medicine, an often-used method of stopping a bleeding wound was cauterization. Taking the flat portion of heated knife blade and placing it directly upon the wound would accomplish this. However, cauterization left deep scar tissue that had no feeling, because it had been rendered insensitive. In the same way, when sin goes unrepented, the conscience loses sensitivity to it. Through continuous resistance toward the Holy Spirit, it becomes increasingly difficult for an individual to come to repentance, because they no longer feel any godly sorrow. They may have some remorse because of the consequences of sinful activity, but not enough to convict them to get on their knees and cry out to God for forgiveness.

SO, WHAT HOPE IS THERE?

"For the word of God is living and powerful, and sharper than any two-edged sword, piercing even to the division of soul and spirit, and of joints and marrow, and is a discerner of the thoughts and intents of the heart" (Hebrews 4:12).

The power of the Word of God is inexpressible in human terms. The Scriptures are the very breath of God and as such are very accurate, defining, and perfectly sufficient (see 2 Timothy 3:16). This is why we begin The Cleansing Stream Seminar with so much of the Word. Scripture reading and study is essential to begin to break down the hardness of the heart that has come about through a gradual searing of the conscience.

In the Old Testament sacrificial system, the blood of the offering was sprinkled on the tabernacle and its vessels in order to sanctify them, making them fit for service. *"Then likewise he sprinkled with blood both the tabernacle and all the vessels of the ministry"* (Hebrews 9:21).

In like manner, as we avail ourselves of the blood of Jesus Christ—the perfect and final sacrifice—our conscience is cleansed, and we become sensitive to the prompting of the Holy Spirit. As the living Word of God begins to awaken our heart and cleanse our conscience, we are drawn by the love of God to again serve Him faithfully. The Word of God awakens and illuminates—the blood of Jesus thoroughly cleanses.

"Let us draw near with a true heart in full assurance of faith, having our hearts sprinkled from an evil conscience and our bodies washed with pure water" (Hebrews 10:22).

"How much more shall the blood of Christ, who through the eternal Spirit offered Himself without spot to God, cleanse your conscience from dead works to serve the living God?" (Hebrews 9:14).

If we fail to prepare someone for deliverance, we may be wasting our time. People can be dragged to the altar, but they can't be made to repent. True repentance comes through the illumination and conviction of the Holy Spirit through the Word of God. Without conviction, there can be no godly sorrow; without godly sorrow there will be no repentance. When there is no repentance, there will be no true deliverance.

Deliverance is not something that can be formulized. Simply following a routine of saying this and doing that will not bring true deliverance. Jesus is the Deliverer. If we will not come to Jesus on His terms, we are only playacting. We might put on a good show, but it will be without substance, and we will only be mocking the Word.

Having said that, let us assume that the person coming for deliverance is convicted of sin and truly wants to be delivered out of their bondage. One of our first goals is to help people understand that they don't need to go through a prayer line to receive deliverance. Jesus is true to His Word, and anyone seeking Him in a right spirit with the right "tools" will experience His freeing power. One such tool we teach is summed up in the phrase "repent, renounce, and break."

REPENT

Let's look at the first word: repent. Breaking this powerful little word apart, we see that it literally means "again (re) humble (penitent)." One who is penitent expresses humble or regretful pain or sorrow for sins or offenses. To repent means to come back to that place of humility and sorrow over sin. We are coming back to the One who grants forgiveness. We are not trying something new or different—we are reaffirming our need for the Savior, Deliverer, and Redeemer, Jesus.

"Nor is there salvation in any other, for there is no other name under heaven given among men by which we must be saved" (Acts 4:12). If there is no repentance, then we continue to walk in darkness, deceived by the enemy. And, if we continue to be deceived, we remain in bondage.

"Therefore say to the house of Israel, 'This is what the Sovereign LORD says: Repent! Turn from your idols and renounce all your detestable practices!'" (Ezekiel 14:6, NIV).

RENOUNCE

To renounce means "to give up, refuse, or resign by formal declaration." Whereas repenting is directed toward God, renouncing is directed toward the enemy. We are countermanding any words or curses (e.g., anything that contradicts God's Word). We are making a formal declaration that we will no longer align ourselves with things that oppose God. We are canceling any and all agreements with the enemy.

Our words are significant, but God has given us authority in Jesus' name to cancel any spiritually binding contract. Many believers repent of their sins before God, only to find themselves in a losing tug-of-war with the enemy, repeating their failures. We must shut the door on the devil, refusing by formal declaration to walk in the ways of the past. Renouncing is the means by which we cut off any legal right for Satan to bind or torment us. This is the way we resist him.

If our words are contrary to God's, then we have aligned ourselves with the works of darkness. To be free from the works of darkness, we must counter those words with God's Word, thus renouncing the hidden works of shame.

"But we have renounced the hidden things of shame, not walking in craftiness nor handling the word of God deceitfully, but by manifestation of the truth commending ourselves to every man's conscience in the sight of God" (2 Corinthians 4:2).

"The night is far spent, the day is at hand. Therefore let us cast off the works of darkness, and let us put on the armor of light" (Romans 13:12).

BREAK

"'For it shall come to pass in that day,' says the LORD of hosts, 'That I will break his yoke from your neck, and will burst your bonds; foreigners shall no more enslave them'" (Jeremiah 30:8).

"It shall come to pass in that day that his burden will be taken away from your shoulder, and his yoke from your neck, and the yoke will be destroyed because of the anointing oil" (Isaiah 10:27, KJV).

Once we repent, we have the right to cancel or renounce any legal hold the enemy had over us—the yoke of bondage can be broken off our lives. God loves to see us come to the place where yokes are broken—and it thoroughly frustrates the enemy!

It is quite common to use anointing oil when praying for someone's deliverance. There is nothing supernatural about the oil. It is, however, significant not of something, but of Someone— who is *very* supernatural. That One is Jesus, the Messiah, the Anointed One (Isaiah 61:1). When we apply oil, it is a point of reference to build faith. We are declaring that repentance has taken place, the enemy has been renounced, and now, with the authority of Jesus' name and because of the power of His death and resurrection, the yoke of bondage is broken (*"...the yoke shall be destroyed because of the anointing"* Isaiah 10:27). At this point of breaking, a struggle begins and ends. It is the primary place of confrontation with the enemy, and now the light of Jesus is shining where darkness once ruled. The enemy has been found out and cast out. It is a great time of freedom and joy. I have seen multiplied thousands of people set free by this simple application of God's Word.

KNOWING OUR AUTHORITY

"For the weapons of our warfare are not carnal but mighty in God for pulling down strongholds" (2 Corinthians 10:4).

It is crucially important for believers going into battle to be aware of their authority in Christ. Deliverance is not a benign activity. We are dealing with disobedient spirits. These demons will use any opportunity to bluff, intimidate, lie, or oppose.

I once received a frantic call. It was 10:00 P.M. and we were about to go to bed. A college student from our church was on the other end of the line. She and another girl had gone to the local pizza parlor next to a University to witness. While they were sitting at their table, a man sat down next to them. He had them somewhat cornered and was scaring them with his words. He was bragging that he had murdered people. One of them had somehow found an excuse to go to the bathroom and had placed the call to

If the Christian warrior is fearful
or unsure of their authority,
they will be exposed and exploited
by the enemy.

me for help. He was acting so strangely that they were convinced he was demon-possessed. My wife and I prayed, and I left quickly for the pizza parlor. When I arrived the place was fairly full. Sitting off to one side was a table with two very scared looking college students and one very ominous man. I sat down next to him. He had a shaved head and an unshaven face. There was a scar on his neck from one ear to the other. If you ever wanted a prototype of a demon-possessed, half-crazed individual, he was it. I no sooner sat down than he scooted his chair close to mine, brought his face within six inches of mine and said in a husky voice, "I don't like you! I think I will kill you—I've killed others!"

Surprising myself I said firmly, "No you won't. In the name of Jesus get back!" At this point he, along with his chair, literally flew back ten feet against the wall. He shook himself and said, "How did you do that?" I said, "It was not me, it was Jesus Christ, and you will obey Him! Now be quiet and leave these people alone." At that point my concern was for the safety of the young girls who promptly left and returned to their dorms.

I have very little faith in my own ability. But I know Jesus, and I am convinced that when He said that He was giving us authority, He was telling the truth.

"And these signs will follow those who believe: In My name they will cast out demons; they will speak with new tongues" (Mark 16:17).

Jesus commended the centurion who simply believed that if Jesus gave the word, his servant would be healed. This centurion understood authority and knew the power of the One giving the healing command.

"'When Jesus heard it, He marveled, and said to those who followed, 'Assuredly, I say to you, I have not found such great faith, not even in Israel!'" (Matthew 8:10).

We must also understand and believe in this authority. It is not a haughty authority, but a humble honest response to who Jesus is and what He has done. The reason we stop our car when a police

Our authority is not derived from our own strength, but rather from the One who granted it to us. Our authority is no less because we're new at it, or because we're young, or frail, or not very wise. Spiritual authority depends not upon us, but upon Him.

car flashes its lights is not because of who's inside, but rather what they represent. The officer in that car may be on the job for the first day. They might be slight of build. They might not be feeling well. Yet, if those lights flash, we stop. Why? They are representing the law. They are coming in the name of the law. If we resist, we are resisting to our own calamity. The entire judicial system will back them up.

Deliverance prayer is so different from what people are used to. Normally, when praying for someone else we close our eyes, bow our head, and speak words of encouragement and blessing. When praying deliverance, our eyes are wide open, looking at the one to whom we're ministering, watching for any signs of struggle, sorrow, anger, etc. The focus of our words is not toward God, but rather a frontal attack against the enemy. We are coming against whatever demon has deceived and manipulated the one in front of us. This is a brand new experience for many.

THE MAD DOG

During our training sessions for those being prepared to minister at a Regional Retreat, we explain the authoritative tone of warfare prayer with this word-picture: imagine a child that you love standing in front of you. Now picture a ravenous dog, snarling and bearing its teeth, approaching to harm this little child. How would you respond? Would you gently say, "Go away, little dog. Please don't bother us."? Would you simply wave your hand at it and go on walking? No, certainly not. Most of us would look for a rock or a stick, and with a loud voice threaten the dog with violence. We'd pick up the child and defend her with our life, if necessary. We would rise up with boldness and be quite unlike our usual self.

In the very same way demons have ravaged God's people. Like mad dogs, they have sought to steal, kill, and destroy. A righteous anger is appropriate when coming against such evil forces. Boldness to confront and put to flight is quite in order. I'm not speaking about volume, but rather a focused and assertive intensity—looking the enemy in the face, making it clear that you know your authority in Christ, and will accept no compromise. The demon *must* leave!

FIGHTING TOGETHER

It is wonderful for me to see the Body of Christ come together in this way. During our Regional Retreats, there may be forty to sixty different congregations represented at one Retreat. Men and women, young and old, people from the pew and pastors from the pulpit, all coming together for one purpose—to see God's people set free. What a thrilling and joyful sight.

This has been one of the great by-products of this ministry. The very nature by which we operate requires that the various congregations going through The Cleansing Stream Seminar all meet together in one place for the Regional Retreat. But something wonderful happens. It appears that Father God takes great joy in family reunions. It greatly pleases Him when His children work and play together. I have a loving family. My wife, Karen, our three children (who for the most part are grown), their spouses and children are all very close. From time to time we have the privilege of all being together. It thrills my heart to see them loving and caring for one another. Unity is wonderful to behold. It seems that the Lord goes out of His way to demonstrate His approval when such unity takes place. And where His presence is, there is also great power. That power is manifested as His people are set free.

Chapter Nine

PRESS TOWARD THE GOAL

I press toward the goal for the prize of the
upward call of God in Christ Jesus.
PHILIPPIANS 3:14

CONTINUING THE JOURNEY

We live in a "bottom line" culture. We have been schooled to want the quick fix, the final answer, the bare facts. Why? So we can do what we need to do and get on to the next thing. Unfortunately, this idea has also permeated the Church, even the way in which we approach freedom in Christ. We want God to break the power of darkness over our lives, and then we want to move on to the next thing, without ever having to think about it again. It doesn't work that way though, because walking with God doesn't work that way. Christianity is a journey, a chance to walk each day dependent upon the Father. In the wake of His powerful, liberating breakthrough in our lives, we must *press on* to a continual surrendering of our hearts to His working, and this involves keeping our lives holy in His sight.

Over the past two years, I've been having an increasingly difficult time with my voice. Finally, I went to a specialist. I had strained my vocal chords. Part of his instructions to me included gargling with warm salt water, once in the morning and once at night. "By the way," he said, "I want you to do this *for the rest of your life.*" There was something very ominous about the words "the rest of your life." Yet, if I wanted to remain healthy, I needed to make some lifestyle changes.

Likewise, deliverance cannot simply become a good program we experience. If it does, and if we fail to address those things that opened the door to spiritual darkness, then bondage will be repeated. To help people establish new habits that will enable them to remain spiritually healthy, our ministry developed a fifth session following the ministry weekend called, "Press Toward the Goal." The purpose of this session is to encourage individuals to

Deliverance is not a program—
it is a lifestyle.

keep practicing the truths and disciplines they learned prior to and during their time of deliverance.

As part of continuing the journey, some go through the Seminar and Retreat again to further establish those truths and gain a greater freedom. Still others use it as a periodic checkup for ongoing cleansing. Because the real bottom line is that to maintain freedom, there must be a willingness to change.

OLD HABITS AND NEW

Preparation *for* deliverance and follow-up *after* deliverance are equally important. Someone delivered from alcohol does not walk into liquor stores. A man who has been addicted to pornography doesn't frequent adult video stores. Changes must be made or bondage is likely to reassert itself. It isn't easy to make these changes. In fact, they can be inexpressibly difficult. But those who want to enjoy the freedom of the Lord, must be willing to do whatever it takes to keep themselves on the path of integrity, accountability, and purity.

As men and women begin their walk with Christ, and as they experience the delivering hand of God, the result is an entirely new lifestyle. One of the most wonderful transformations took place in the life of a man called John, from California.

THE MIRACLE OF A CHANGED LIFE

Jesus' love for each of us is truly awesome! He reached down and touched the heart of a precious homeless man named John. After accepting Jesus as his Savior through a homeless ministry, he was baptized and then attended a class on the fundamentals of Christian faith. God set him free from alcohol and started using him to help other homeless men and women. Seeing the dramatic change in his life, they all began to want what he had—Jesus! The power of God had delivered John, and the radical lifestyle changes that followed, enabled God to continue a good work in his life.

John and his blind friend, James, knew of a homeless man who was in the hospital in a coma. They went with others to the hospital to pray and anoint the man with oil. In answer to their fervent prayers, the Lord healed that man and brought him out of the coma. After months of preparation in The Cleansing Stream Seminar, John attended a Regional Retreat. Jesus met him in a special way as He wants to do for each of us. A song of joy kept going through his mind, and he couldn't stop singing it! There was a real glow on his face, and he said he felt truly cleansed.

John gave his testimony to over 100 men and women at the homeless ministry the following Wednesday night. He shared what the Lord had done for him through The Cleansing Stream Seminar and Regional Retreat. As a result, many homeless people followed John's example, considering him a leader, and John is following Jesus! Praise the Lord for this changed vessel. John was a changed man and, as a result, everything around him changed. Yes, he changed some old habits—but just as importantly, he made some new ones.

CLEANING HOUSE

When speaking of cleaning house, I am, of course, referring to more than using a vacuum cleaner and dust rag. I am talking about our spiritual houses; we are the temple of the Holy Spirit. Once delivered, we must keep our "home" clean by getting rid of old habits and ungodly attachments. 1 Corinthians 6:19 reminds us, *"Or do you not know that your body is the temple of the Holy Spirit who is in you, whom you have from God, and you are not your own?"* What we allow to go into our minds and hearts makes a difference in our ability, our sensitivity, to God's liberating work in our lives.

King David realized this and declared, *"I will set nothing wicked before my eyes"* (Psalm 101:3). It is up to us to keep a vigilant watch over our souls. There are many things that can give entrance to demonic influence, some of them seemingly harmless. By saying this, I do not mean to stir up fear or condemnation; rather, I hope to stir up thoughtful evaluation of the things in your home and in your life that might reopen a door to spiritual darkness. When uncertain about whether or not a certain item, activity, or relationship is harmful to our spiritual growth we can pray and ask, *Will this pollute my mind and heart?* If the answer is yes, then we must take steps to shut the door to that darkness and bar its influence in our life.

To begin, get rid of any objects in your house connected to your past that could draw you back into sin, or that are in and of themselves ungodly. For example, I left the occult as a young man after having come to Christ. Accordingly, I took all the books I had revered and studied, along with jewelry and art connected with that demonic activity, and destroyed them. Sound extreme? It really isn't. In fact, the book of Acts describes a similar response from new believers who wanted to completely disassociate themselves from their past and become devoted followers of Jesus (see Acts 19:18-20). Part of staying free is keeping our homes cleansed from items of sinful activity.

I once received a frantic call from a family in our congregation. She and her husband had been living in terror for a couple of weeks, and they needed help. Their five-year-old daughter had been behaving quite strangely. At night they would hear her speaking with what they first thought was an imaginary friend. Her voice was always frightened, and several times she had screamed. When they went into her room, it was literally cold—almost down to freezing temperature.

When I arrived, I asked the parents who owned the house prior to them. The mother explained that the house was originally owned by her parents, and the room in which her little girl slept was once her own. I asked her if she had ever dabbled in the occult. "Oh no!" she said. "I have been a Christian most of my life and I knew better than to do such things." "Ever?" I inquired again. She pondered her past and then explained, "Well, once my girlfriend and I played with a Ouija board. It actually began to move, and it so scared us that we stopped immediately and threw out the board." "How old were you?" I asked. "I was the same age as my daughter is now," she replied.

Immediately, she saw the connection. "You opened a door." I said. "The enemy is a legalist and will use every opportunity to gain a strategic hold." We prayed together. The mother confessed her sin, asked God's forgiveness, and renounced all binding agreements with the enemy. We then went into their daughter's bedroom, anointed the walls and door, praying throughout the room. That was the last of the troublesome manifestations.

Our home isn't the only place we need to search for possible ungodly attachments. Consider your place of work and/or ministry. What changes should take place in your work environment? Are there any relationships that need to be altered? Though we do not have complete control over everything that goes on in our workplace, we can control what we will participate in. By guarding our conversations and our commitments, we can keep the door closed to sin. This may mean significant changes in present friendships and acquaintances. It may mean cutting off people who carry a great deal of prestige and power. But walking in freedom requires that we are willing to change our old ways and forge new ones by His grace.

RELEASED TO SERVE

All of this scrutiny can appear to make us very self-focused. The question needs to be asked, "*Why* am I doing this?" Deliverance isn't selfish, though, it is restoring us to live as God intended. Certainly at our Retreats there is great joy as we worship our great and awesome God. There is also great joy as we lay hands on the oppressed, watching multitudes set free. It isn't just emotionalism, though there is great emotion behind it. It isn't just a "give me" group of people with no heart to serve, waiting only for the next new thrill. For the most part, those involved in deliverance ministry are sincere, godly men and women—many of whom were at first skeptical—rejoicing in the loving graciousness of their Lord. What do we do with all of this newfound freedom? Once the oppressed are unburdened, what then?

A necessary aspect of the journey is setting a new focus. It is the voice of Jesus saying to the once leprous, *"...Go, show yourselves to the priests..."* (Luke 17:14, NIV), in order that they could become witnesses of Jesus as Messiah. It is the woman at the well, now free, who runs back into town to bring a city to Jesus (see John 4). And in our day, it is the man who felt so useless, especially to God, now set free from the spirit of rejection, ready to serve God. Many who have participated in The Cleansing Stream Seminar and Retreat have gone back through, helping others walk to freedom. Others have been asked by pastoral leadership to be trained to minister deliverance in The Cleansing Stream Discipleship Seminar. Still others, now better equipped, move into service in the local church.

Deliverance is indeed an amazing thing. It releases us to be vibrant witnesses of the love and power of God. Time and again pastors report to me that people in their church who were once pew-sitters are now seeking ways in which to serve. Jeremiah had it right when he said, *"Therefore this is what the LORD says: 'If you repent, I will restore you that you may serve me'"* (15:19, NIV).

Chapter Ten

DEVELOPING
DISCIPLES

And the things that you have heard from me
among many witnesses, commit these to faithful
men who will be able to teach others also.
2 TIMOTHY 2:2

Deliverance is not meant to be a program, but rather an every-day occurrence in the life of the local church. This will never happen, though, until we understand the need to train others in deliverance who, in turn, will train the next line in the rank. The necessity of carrying along God's truth to future generations cannot be understated. All of us who call ourselves Christian do so because of the faithfulness of previous generations to promote the gospel of Jesus Christ. Deliverance is no different. There has always been a remnant that understood deliverance; it has always been passed along somehow. Yet God is doing something different in our day. The Church must be ready to minister to the multitudes that are receiving Christ. One of the first things Jesus Christ did during His earthly ministry was cleanse the temple (see John 2:12-16.). Now, in these last days, He has come again to cleanse His Church. There is a special anointing upon this season to restore God's plan to the Church for setting captives free. Discipleship training in the ministry of deliverance is an essential part of getting this back into the Church.

To effectively prepare people to minister deliverance, there needs to be a sensible plan in place. In The Cleansing Stream Discipleship Seminar we call this "Teaching, Training, and Touching." Eliminating any one of these will result in ineffective discipleship.

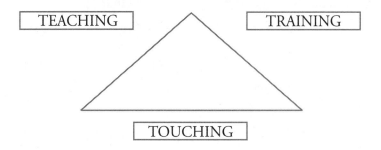

TEACHING

Many leaders have seen the grievous result of giving authority to an immature Christian, or to one with wrong motives. I would never place a sword in the hands of a four-year old boy, because he is likely to remove a limb or two before long. Raising up people to minister in the area of deliverance first requires laying a solid foundation that establishes fundamental biblical truths. The first year of this training is focused on planting the disciple firmly upon the Word of God.

The first step emphasizes the need to know "who He is and who we are." Putting Jesus first is essential for every minister. Deliverance has a way of attracting the strange and goofy people who love to be the center of attention. The enemy loves to see someone caught up with the authority they have. It quickly lends itself to pride and elitism. To avoid this, every disciple must remain accountable. Certain rules are laid down for their benefit and safety:

1.   No one being trained is permitted to minister deliverance alone.
2.   All deliverance sessions must be conducted by a team of people led by a trained team leader.
3.   All deliverance sessions must be done with the pastor's full knowledge and approval.
4.   A follow-up report will be provided to the pastor.
5.   Any individual conducting deliverance on their own and those conceding to separatist or secret ministry will be removed from the discipleship training for a period of time determined by the pastor and team leader.
6.   Violating confidentiality is also grounds for being removed from the team.

The reason for these rules, and for the strict enforcement of accountability, is to protect discipleship seminar team members from the greatest seduction of the enemy: pride. Pride quickly leads to heresy. Unchecked by strict boundaries, the enemy will be sure to steer the disciple toward the more "mystical" aspects of the demonic.

Understanding the importance of holiness is another key to successful ministry. It is so important that our hearts be right before God. We continually encourage those we train to consider their motives. Are they involved in deliverance ministry because it feeds some fallen aspect of their nature? Do they truly have a servant attitude? Do they see others as more important than themselves? Are they seeking to gain or to give?

As a pastor, I would much rather have someone serve who had the fruit of the Spirit, but no active spiritual gifts, than someone who functioned with the gifts, but had no fruit (see Galatians 5:22-23 and 1 Corinthians 12:1-7). The techniques of deliverance play a

Gleaning information by conversing with demons and/or becoming absorbed with fallen angelic hierarchies are just some of the so-called "secret" mysteries that intoxicate the immature deliverance minister.

very small part in training disciples. If the heart is right, the "how to" is simple to explain.

TRAINING

In 1964, I went through Army boot camp at Ft. Polk, Louisiana. Less than two years from then, I would be in Vietnam. Two events stand out in my mind as a part of our training. One was dodging live ammo during an assault exercise. We had to crawl one hundred feet under barbed wire with live machine gun rounds firing a couple of feet over our heads. The other was entering a wood shack filled with tear gas. We had masks on, but our drill sergeant stepped up and commanded us individually to remove the mask and shout out our serial number. Inevitably, if we failed to shout loud enough, we were required to shout it out again. By that time we had to take a breath—and, oh boy, there is nothing like a lung and eye full of tear gas. What we learned in the classroom was then put into practice during the training exercise, and from there it would be taken onto the battlefield.

Training provides the disciple with the practical tools needed to walk people to freedom. It moves each one from Bible study to hands-on experience. Generally, those going through our training method (The Cleansing Stream Discipleship Seminar), are meeting in a local church under a team leader. As a group, they meet two or three times a month. One week they watch a training video, and another week they pray for each other in a particular area for deliverance. No one is ever exempt from being prayed for. The point of training is giving an opportunity to put the teaching into action—and what better place to use it than with others who are a part of the discipleship training team? Deliverance is a process. The further on we walk with the Lord, the more we should be open to be prayed for. Let me share an example from my own life.

WALKING IN THE LIGHT

It was a winter evening in New York. I had just finished eating dinner and stepped outside to catch a taxi to my hotel. When none were to be found, I began to walk toward a nearby, brightly lit hotel where I thought I might be able to find some transportation. Just then, a car passed by, splashing me with muddy water. I couldn't see how muddy because of the poor lighting, but at the time it didn't seem too bad. As I walked closer to the light I began see just how badly I was splashed. By the time I reached the hotel I could see everything clearly—I was a mess!

The longer I am a Christian, the more I recognize my need of the Cross. The closer I walk to the light, the more clearly I see my need for cleansing and forgiveness. And the further I go on my journey with the Lord, the more I understand my need for deliverance. I am not speaking about my eternal salvation—that was settled when I received Christ as my Savior. But the Christian life is a journey, a process, and throughout our lives we are being sanctified. Those who walk in darkness do not see their deplorable state. Like walking in a mud-stained coat, they don't realize just how dirty their lives are. It's only when they come to the light that they see their true condition. The older I get, the more I appreciate God's mercy and grace. Hebrews 10:14 tells us: *"For by one offering He has perfected forever those who are being sanctified."* What a great verse! I have the assurance of my salvation in my *spirit*—having been perfected forever—and I keep on moving toward that perfection—being sanctified in my *soul*—as the Holy Spirit is working in me.

For this reason, we require that each team member be open to receive deliverance prayer at any time.

TOUCHING

The teaching and training are for the purpose of preparing the disciple to be confident in leading someone through deliverance. The opportunities for deliverance take place in two venues. One is the Cleansing Stream Regional Retreat. As mentioned before, many churches that have been conducting The Cleansing Stream Seminar come together. The Retreats provide an excellent opportunity for those being trained in The Cleansing Stream Discipleship Seminar to directly minister to many people, and, in the process, gain more training from more experienced leaders. The other venue is their local church, and I will discuss this opportunity more fully in the next chapter.

At our Retreats, we have what is called the "line." It is on the line where ministry takes place. I am thrilled as I watch men and women, young and old, joyfully ministering to their brothers and sisters in Christ. It gets the people off the pew and literally onto the front line of action. They get to lovingly care for many hurting people and do battle against demonic forces. It is a place of love and war, of tenderness and toughness. Just about every emotion is witnessed. Both the head and the heart have to be alert. The gifts of the Spirit are operational, and the fruit of the Spirit is manifested. Men and women, who before may have been passive in the pew, experience a sense of fulfillment as they become of great service to Christ.

We receive hundreds of testimonies every year from those who have received ministry. There is no greater joy than to hear their words of gratitude and joy for the ones whom God had used. Here's a letter that beautifully sums up this sentiment:

"I think you have listened and discerned well! As a spiritual director involved in a healing ministry, I wonder if one reason Cleansing Stream Ministries is so blessed with deliverance and healing results, is due to the fact that you bring each participant directly to Christ and His healing Spirit—no earthly 'middle man' is needed! Christ receives all the glory! The corporate setting creates community and calls down a huge anointing. You've established a safe, caring, non-judgmental atmosphere (amongst strangers!) for deliverance and inner healing to take its place in individuals. Amazing Grace! Only God could have put this much of Himself into giving this much freedom to so many. You have listened and discerned well indeed!"

CHOSEN AND COMMITTED

I cannot overemphasize the importance of the word "chosen." For deliverance in the local church to operate smoothly, there must be pastoral or proven, mature leaders involved in covering and leading the ministry. This is especially true when it comes to those who will be appointed to go through deliverance training, and eventually be laying hands on others.

First, the pastor or leader prays and asks the Lord for wisdom as to whom to invite to be trained to minister deliverance. One guideline to consider first is choosing those who have been through The Cleansing Seminar and Retreat—maybe even a few times. You only want those who have experienced personal cleansing themselves to lay hands on others for the same. And yet, as a pastor, I knew that even though someone had received deliverance, it didn't automatically qualify him or her for this ministry. The pastor or leader must be sure and confident of those who are asked to serve.

Once a list has been made of potential trainees, it is wise to meet with them individually. I strongly advise that if married, the husband and wife join in the training together. This is not always possible, though, and should not become an absolute requirement. When meeting with them, the pastor or leader should go over the details of the commitment of time, finances, etc. On the following page, I have included a form that is used in The Cleansing Discipleship Seminar to give an idea of what types of questions to ask and what information to cover.

It might appear from this form that only those who are perfect may apply. That's not the case at all. We consider this something that a disciple should be aspiring toward, rather than be perfected in.

A MATTER OF CONFIDENCE

Those who wish to minister in the area of deliverance must be fully committed to confidentiality—*no exceptions or excuses!* It doesn't hurt to repeat this obligation several times to potential candidates. The ministry of deliverance will flounder and fail quickly if confidentiality is shaky. Before and after any deliverance session, the prayer team is reminded that what has taken place is not to be disclosed. Any violation of this rule results in immediate removal.

CLEANSINGSTREAM   CSD Training Commitment Agreement
MINISTRIES®

(Must be renewed annually)

CS Discipleship Philosophy – CS Discipleship training is for maturing believers approved by their pastor and church leadership. Each potential participant must be aware that once they commit to CS Discipleship training, they are taking a stand on the front lines of the spiritual battle. They are saying in effect, "Lord Jesus, teach me spiritual warfare." CS Discipleship training is designed to span two (2) years, each year consisting of an eleven (11) month training period.

Points of Commitment   CS Discipleship Training Period – Starts: ____/____ Ends: ____/____

Personally I commit to:
- Walk in humility, transparency, and accountability to my pastor, church leadership , and CSD leader(s)
- Be teachable, correctable, and willing to be discipled
- Be a team player always striving for unity
- Be trustworthy and hold confidentiality of those to whom I minister (violating confidentiality is grounds for suspension from CSD)
- Maintain a disciplined life of prayer, praise, and daily Bible devotionals
- If married, maintain a strong and unified relationship with my spouse (it is strongly recommended that both spouses participate in the training)

In my church, I commit to:
- Remain submitted under the covering of my church and pastor
- Fully embrace and support the vision for my church as formulated by my pastor and church leadership
- Maintain regular church membership, attendance, and consistent tithing
- Continue in my church ministry responsibilities

While in CSD training, I commit to:
- Attend all the teaching and training sessions as outlined by my CSD Coordinator
- Participate on an assigned CSD Prayer Team at least one additional time per month for further training, personal deliverance ministry, prayer, and fellowship
- Commit to pursuing on-going personal cleansing in my life by submitting to deliverance prayer by my local CSD team at least once a year
- Minister with love and sensitivity to the people assigned to my team for prayer
- Complete all assigned homework, which includes:
    - Completing all session workbooks as outlined by my CSD leader(s)
    - Studying the session books/audiotapes
    - Fast one day per week
    - Pray daily for my team members and team leaders
- Participate in two (2) Cleansing Seminar Retreats during the discipleship year, at least one of which will be a CSM Regional Retreat
- When ministering at a CSM Retreat, I will submit to CSM Retreat leadership
- Abide by the CSD Prayer and Ministry Guidelines, when not with my team, which state:
    - Limit my personal prayer and ministry to prayers of encouragement, comfort, and exhortation; continued revelation of a person's need, strengthening of a person's will; and healing
    - Determine the person's need for salvation, water baptism, etc. and encourage his/her participation in the established services and ministries at the church
    - If the need for deliverance is discerned, I will refer the person to my CSD Coordinator. **In other words, until I am released by my pastor and my CSD Coordinator, I am not free (at any time or in any place) to minister deliverance without the approval and presence of my team leader.**
- To comply with the CSD Guidelines regarding Traveling/Visiting Deliverance Ministries (other than those held in my church), including:
    - As I go, I am not representing my church or the CSD Team at my church
    - I will not take anyone with me for ministry who is being ministered to by the CSD teams or another ministry in my church
    - I will advise my CSD Team Leader/Coordinator prior to attending ·

MY COMMITMENT

I have **read**, I **understand**, and I **am committed** to fulfill all the objectives of the Cleansing Stream Discipleship Mission Statement and to abide by the Ministry Guidelines. I commit to this **eleven month** (11-month) **discipling training period**, and I agree to adjust my current ministry responsibilities and personal schedule accordingly so that I am able to participate fully in this training.

Participant Signature	___/___/___ **Date**	For married participants, each spouse must complete and sign a CSD Training Application and CSD Commitment Agreement form.

Note: See pages 17 & 18 of the "*CSD Leadership Manual*" for copies of this Application and Agreement form. They must be given to and signed by each CSD Participant.

MAKE SURE YOU COMPLETE AND SIGN BOTH PAGES/SIDES OF THIS FORM AND RETURN TO YOUR CSD COORDINATOR.

CSD Training Composite Form – Part "A" –Training Commitment Agreement.pdf, © 2001-2002 Cleansing Stream Ministries, Inc., Rev. 02/12/02

Reprinted with permission.

© Cleansing Stream Ministries

NO LONE RANGERS

Deliverance in the church is most effective as a team effort. This maintains accountability and avoids the trap of pride. I remember Apostle John Eckhardt telling a story relating to this issue. In their church, they practice team prayer. One night at about two o'clock in the morning, Apostle Eckhardt answered his phone. A member of his congregation was with a friend who asked him if he would pray for him to be delivered from demonic bondage. He began to minister and his friend began to manifest badly. He became quite scared and was now over his head in problems. Frantically, he called his pastor. Apostle Eckhardt said to him, "I told you not to do deliverance on your own. You must work with the church team. Now, you've got yourself into this mess—and you can get yourself out of it." At that point, he hung up the phone and went back to sleep. He said there was a time when he would have jumped into his clothes, got in his car, and sped off to where the wayward member was. But, he decided that lessons had to be learned. You cannot allow for lone rangers in deliverance ministry.

Thankfully, God does not leave us, or those to whom we minister, even when we make foolish choices. His covering is continually upon those who seek him with honest faith. However, He does sometimes let us feel the consequences of our mistakes so that we will grow and mature into people who honor Him. Those who minister in the area of deliverance must be submitted to pastoral authority and accountable to those around them. This ministry is too volatile to be conducted any other way. Working with a team, as we will see in the next chapter, has great value apart from keeping us out of trouble.

Chapter Eleven

TEAM
PRAYER

*For this reason I bow my knees to the Father of our
Lord Jesus Christ, from whom the whole family in
heaven and earth is named, that He would grant you,
according to the riches of His glory, to be strengthened
with might through His Spirit in the inner man, that
Christ may dwell in your hearts through faith; that you,
being rooted and grounded in love, may be able to
comprehend with all the saints what is the width and
length and depth and height—to know the love of Christ
which passes knowledge; that you may be filled with all
the fullness of God.*

EPHESIANS 3:14-19

A man who had great influence upon me was the late Dr. Walter
Martin. Walter was a good friend. Beyond that, he mentored
me for a couple of years. I remember a very poignant statement he
once made to me, "Chris, there is something I want you to always

remember. In Christianity, there are many counterfeits. But whenever you find a counterfeit, you can be sure about one thing. Somewhere out there is the genuine article." I believe this to be true about deliverance. While there have been some truly gifted pioneers in deliverance, the Church has also seen many counterfeits. Like a circus, they roll into town with great fanfare. A three-ring-circus is about to perform! The things you will see will astound you. You will applaud the actors and performers. Such daredevils! Such showmen! Certainly no one else can do the things they do! And when they leave, you'll have the memory—and also have the mess to clean up. Unfortunately, the mess comes in the form of human pain and suffering. For a moment you will be thrilled, but then life goes back to normal and everything is the way it was because generally nothing genuine, or real, took place.

Jesus shunned performance. Whenever He could, He avoided the limelight. He disdains hypocrisy and loathes the selfish ambition after which some seek. And He stands in the midst of the Church today, faithfully speaking His Word to those who will hear. In the midst of all the smoke and mirrors, there *is* the genuine—there is real deliverance.

Is it possible for there to be a biblically balanced approach to casting out demons? Can it be done without humiliating those who are bound and broken? Can it be done in an orderly way in the Church? Is it possible to have this happen with loving, pastoral care? Oh, yes, it certainly is possible—and how I love to see it happen!

My desire is to see the ministry of deliverance established in every local church. This happens most naturally through the inviting of qualified candidates, and the training and establishing of prayer teams as is suggested in The Cleansing Stream Discipleship Seminar. The invitation and training process have been outlined in preceding chapters, but what do these prayer teams look like? And, how do you train them?

Properly trained, mature people in the church can lovingly wage war on behalf of their brothers and sisters in Christ, and do so in an atmosphere of genuine accountability.

Ephesians 3:14-19 is a prayer from the heart of the apostle Paul to see people filled with the fullness of God. Yet, the means by which they get there is often overlooked. It states: *"that you, being rooted and grounded in love."* The catalyst to effective ministry is love. I'm personally convinced that it is this very same love that unravels the cords of hell. It is the love of Christ operating through the disciple of Christ that truly overpowers the enemy and dismantles his fortresses. The enemy has no equal to the love of Jesus Christ. Therefore, the most effective deliverance will be clothed in His love. With love in mind, let's look at an example of what team prayer looks like when it is functioning well.

A TYPICAL MODEL

Let's assume for the moment that there is a particular prayer team—one of four—operating in First City Church. Just how did they get to the place of having four teams? Using the Cleansing Stream model, the local church conducts The Cleansing Stream Seminar (which prepares the participant to *receive* deliverance) twice a year in an ongoing manner. Those who have been through the Seminar and Retreat a couple of times are eligible for The Cleansing Stream Discipleship Seminar (which prepares the participant to *minister* deliverance). The pastor selects those whom he or she feels are qualified to be trained. In groups of six to eight, these people are placed on prayer teams. There would also be a team leader and often a co-leader. This prayer team commitment is for two years. They would meet a minimum of twice a month: once to watch the teaching or training video, and again to pray for team members or a congregational member released by the pastor. In addition, they commit to minister at several Cleansing Stream Regional Retreats.

PROCEDURE

If someone from the congregation needs deliverance prayer, he or she would contact the pastor who would then provide their name and phone number to the team leader. After speaking with the person desiring prayer (the "prayee") in person or by phone, the team leader completes the questionnaire called a Ministry Request Form. I have provided a typical questionnaire as an example on the following page.

From this questionnaire a sense of direction can be discerned. The team leader sets up an appointment time for the prayee to meet with the team for prayer. The team leader, in turn, sends a copy of the form to the pastor, notifying him or her when the deliverance prayer is scheduled and who will be involved. After prayer, a follow-up report is sent to the pastor. All this is kept strictly confidential. (For a more extensive questionnaire sample, see Doris Wagner's book *How to Cast Out Demons*, Regal Books)

PREPARATION
The team meets ahead of time to pray for the deliverance prayer session and to be informed by the team leader regarding the area

Ministry Request Form

Person requesting prayer _____ Phone (AM)_____ (PM)_____
Address_____

Personal Information and History: Married?_____ Salvation Date _____
Water Baptism Date _____ CSS dates ___   _____
Church Info: Member_____ # of Years Attended_____ Consistent Attendance?_____
Areas of service at the church_____
Current involvement in counseling _____
_____ Related medications_____

Deliverance Prayer Needs:
What are they requesting prayer for? (identify areas of continued struggle, failure or sin)_____

_____

_____

_____

_____

History: _personal_—areas of past sin contributing to this area, _generational_—family or relationship difficulties
behind this area_____

_____

_____

_____

How is an attack of the enemy or temptation handled in this area?_____

_____

_____

Recommendations...
...for prayer_____

_____

...for Homework to be completed prior to ministry session_____

_____

Ministry (Prayer) Appointment Information		
Form completed by		Date
Ministry Appointment Date	Time	Location
Team		Ministry Progress Form Completed?

Reprinted by permission from the Cleansing Stream Leader's Guide #3, p. 22
© Cleansing Stream Ministries

for deliverance prayer (based upon the questionnaire and discernment). The team leader gives specific assignments to each of the team members. Some assignments may be shared. Typical assignments would be:

1. A team member to read the Word (proclaiming quietly at certain times and loudly at others);
2. A team member to record Scriptures, prophecies, or important information;
3. A team member to be a loving encourager to the participant;
4. Another team member to do spiritual warfare and intercession during the deliverance session;
5. All team members are assigned to seek the Lord for discernment and revelation;
6. The elements of the deliverance prayer session can also be divided among the team members as follows:
   - One team member would be assigned to lead the participant through any needed prayer to forgive others;
   - Another team member would lead through repentance, confessing their own sin to God;
   - Another team member would lead the person through renouncing;
   - Another team member would lead through the breaking portion of the prayer and so forth.

The team leader may directly participate in any of the above assignments, or decide to simply oversee all that takes place. Some leaders choose to rotate these assignments throughout the course of the deliverance prayer, others stay with one assignment. Either can work effectively.

Preparing the Room

No matter where you meet, it is always wise to pray throughout the room before the participant arrives. Chairs are formed in a circle. The team begins with praise and worship, acknowledging that it is only God who can deliver. The Word is spoken over the room, which is anointed with oil. The team leader will go over the questionnaire to make sure everyone understands the direction of the prayer time. The team leader will then give the assignments.

Greeted With Love

When the person to be prayed for arrives, they are often anxious about what will happen. The number of people on the team can, at first glance, seem intimidating. This can be overcome by the way the team greets and treats the prayee. If they are greeted with love, warmth, and friendliness, it will do much to set at ease any fear or concern.

Additional praise and worship is often appropriate at this beginning time. The team leader leads out in prayer for the Lord to superintend everything that takes place during the deliverance prayer session. The team leader reviews the questionnaire, allowing the prayee to provide any additional information the Lord has revealed since the interview.

Discerning and Delivering

It is wonderful to watch God move in this environment. The prayer team moves in unity, seeks discernment and revelation, hears from God, addresses the enemy, receives revelations of truth, dismantles demonic strongholds, and gives praise and adoration to God.

It is not unusual for there to be manifestations during times of great spiritual struggle, when truth faces lies and where God takes ground back. As in the days of Joshua, the enemy does not like to lose any territory. Although the Promised Land legally belonged to God's people, it required confrontation to secure ownership. Satan doesn't give up ground easily. During the time of deliverance, we assign someone to sit next to the prayee to give encouragement. Their job is to help the individual to resist the enemy, believe God's word, embrace the truth, and reject any further involvement with lying spirits. (I have purposely not gone into great detail describing the actual encounter and suggesting what should be spoken, etc. The Cleansing Stream Discipleship Seminar leadership materials do all of that.)

Following the deliverance prayer session, we encourage the receiving of Communion, being reminded that everything of value that happened occurred because of the Cross of Jesus Christ.

FURTHER CLEANSING

At the end of the session, we often remind the team—in front of the prayee—that everything that took place is under strict confidentiality. After the person leaves, the team leader will then go over the details of the deliverance prayer session, giving opportunity for the team to share insights they received. The leader, if called for, will disciple the team members by offering suggestions for improvement. To conclude, prayer and praise is offered to God, cleansing the room of any demonic residue.

WHY PRAYER TEAMS?

Prayer is a place of growth and blessing for everyone involved—for the ones receiving it and the ones giving it. Through prayer we invite the presence of God to invade our lives and bring the establishment of His Kingdom and will. In the ministry of deliverance, prayer isn't just a part—it is the whole. Because of this, organized and accountable prayer teams are invaluable.

How Does Team Prayer Benefit the Church?

1. Every area of church life is impacted as team members walk out their faith.
2. The number of trained workers in the church increase.
3. Potential conflicts are averted, because trouble spots are quickly discovered and healed.
4. Unity is increased, since a greater number of people learn how to minister together.
5. Leaders continue to mature in their faith.
6. New disciplines are embraced.
7. New leaders are birthed.

How Does Team Prayer Benefit Those Who Are Involved?

1. Participating in ministry enables them to become active in their faith.
2. Opportunities to help someone else are provided.
3. Each member continues to grow in their relationship with the Lord and one another.
4. Ongoing deliverance and healing is received.
5. New disciplines for spiritual growth are learned.
6. The gifts of the Spirit are realized and put into practice.
7. Some prayer team members emerge as leaders within the church.

Without belaboring the point, I hope that you have caught the vision of how prayer teams can provide an avenue for a loving and successful deliverance ministry.

Chapter Twelve

BENEFITS TO
THE CHURCH

*Until we all come to the unity of the faith
and of the knowledge of the Son of God, to a
perfect man, to the measure of the stature of the
fullness of Christ.*
EPHESIANS 4:13

EACH ONE DOES THEIR PART

Knowledge alone has sometimes been erroneously considered maturity. Yet, maturity really happens as one lives and walks out the Christian life. You can't mature just by reading a book; you have to put into practice what you have learned (see Hebrews 5:14). Deliverance flows from an accurate knowledge of the Word of God and the authority He has given His Church for spiritual combat—and in combat you must stay awake and use the training you have received.

I find that those who have themselves been through deliverance in The Cleansing Stream Seminar and Retreat, and now are being trained to minister deliverance in The Cleansing Stream Discipleship Seminar, become a powerful asset to the church body. Immediately following church services, there is often an opportunity for people to come down to the front for prayer. Although we rarely minister deliverance during an open, regularly scheduled meeting, those who are experienced in it, are able to exercise many of the gifts of the Spirit in praying for people. They have greater compassion, and because they have practiced spiritual discernment, they minister to their brothers and sisters with much greater understanding and insight.

In every church there are untapped resources such as this waiting to be brought to light. People who never imagined that they could be of any use to God or anyone else—people who always thought that someone else could do the task better—now become active leaders within the Body of Christ.

In my own congregation, I watched this happen. I saw members who were broken and bruised go through deliverance and sud-

In retrospect, I realized that
this new burst of church life
all came as a result of seeing people delivered
from demonic bondage.

denly come alive in their faith. They were too full of rejection or shame to do anything before—but once they had experienced the cleansing power of God, they wanted to be everything God created them to be. It wasn't long before many of them took on leadership roles. Men who at one time were bored with Christianity got the scent of battle and roared to life. Women who felt boxed in by limited resources or poor education found avenues of freedom they never thought possible and thrived in the newfound bounty.

All of this to say that establishing a ministry of deliverance— recruiting, training, and releasing people to serve—is not just a blessing to those who receive freedom, it is a surge of life that the whole church enjoys. People grow by using their gifts, learning to depend upon the Lord, and lean into Him, and that is what brings the whole Body of Christ to true unity in the faith. The saints, the family of God, must step into their place and minister to those around them—especially those called to minister in the area of deliverance.

SHARING AND EXTENDING THE CHURCH'S VISION

When implemented rightly, the ministry of deliverance does not become the focal point of the church. That means providing the following: (1) preparation for deliverance (like The Cleansing Stream Seminar), (2) a place to receive deliverance (like the Cleansing Stream Regional Retreats and prayer teams within the local church), and (3) preparation for maturing Christians to receive discipleship in ministering deliverance (like The Cleansing Stream Discipleship Seminar). When first starting up, it may seem like it is a focal point, but over time it moves to the background and becomes just another thread in the tapestry. And that's what it should be, because nothing should steal from the vision set forth by the pastor and leaders, providing that the Head over it all is Jesus Christ. My experience, and that of hundreds of other pastors, is that deliverance ministry produces new leaders who can come alongside their pastor and share in the vision for their local church. Men and women, who have a heart for their city, can work alongside their pastor to see their city won for Christ. They are evangelistic, they work with kids in the poorer part of town, they teach Sunday School, they join in intercessory prayer—because they are excited about their faith and want to share with others what God has done for them.

DECREASING THE COUNSELING LOAD

"And He Himself gave some to be apostles, some prophets, some evangelists, and some pastors and teachers, for the equipping of the saints for the work of ministry, for the edifying of the body of Christ" (Ephesians 4:11-12).

Once we had implemented deliverance ministry and prayer teams (using the two Cleansing Stream Seminars), things in our church changed dramatically. I used to spend many hours a week counseling with those in the congregation. Then, I began asking those coming for help to attend The Cleansing Stream Seminar. Then, if further help was needed, they could come see me. Most of those who attended the Seminar and Retreat didn't require further counseling. Those who did were referred to a prayer team leader, who, in turn, set up a deliverance prayer session with a Cleansing Stream Discipleship team.

The net result was that my counseling load decreased by about sixty percent. The Body was ministering to the Body—it was doing the work of the ministry! Most every pastor desires to "equip the saints for the work of the ministry." But in many church circles, it seems to work the other way—the saints want the *pastor* equipped to do the work of the ministry. The only way all the work can get done, though, is if the saints are equipped and serving others.

Our call from God at Cleansing Stream Ministries, includes a clear mandate to work within the framework of the local church.

But again, I want to acknowledge that there are proven parachurch ministries and missionary organizations that are being used of God in effective deliverance ministry.

LOVING THE BRIDE

"I will greatly rejoice in the LORD, my soul shall be joyful in my God; for He has clothed me with the garments of salvation, He has covered me with the robe of righteousness, as a bridegroom decks himself with ornaments, and as a bride adorns herself with her jewels" (Isaiah 61:10).

Marriage is love and intimacy. It is commitment and sacrifice. It is honor and respect. It's no wonder the Lord would choose this metaphor to describe the relationship between Himself and the Church. He wants this type of intimacy with His people—a vulnerable and faithful devotion that enriches and blesses. The book of Ephesians says it well:

"Husbands, love your wives, just as Christ also loved the church and gave Himself for her, that He might sanctify and cleanse her with the washing of water by the word, that He might present her to Himself a glorious church, not having spot or wrinkle or any such thing, but that she should be holy and without blemish" (5:25-27).

As we examine this passage of Scripture, we see how the Lord views us. He regards us the way a bridegroom regards his bride. Can there be anything more tender and passionate? Song of Solomon 4:7 echoes this cry, *"You are all fair, my love, and there is no spot in you."*

Scripture is replete with verses both from the perspective of the bridegroom as well as the bride, and all of them point to God's desire to share a life of love with His chosen people, His bride.

I can recall as if it were yesterday watching *my* bride, Karen, walk down the isle on our wedding day. She was beautiful then, and more beautiful now. I would give my life for her, and she would do the same for me. We are one—and have been so for over thirty-two years as of the writing of this book.

Karen and I made an agreement in the first year of our marriage. Neither of us would ever ridicule nor in any way demean the other. We would never put one another down in public. Now, you don't go through thirty-two years of marriage without some severe ups and downs, and we have had our share. Arguments, disagreements, and reconciliation have each had their season in our marital journey. This is not uncommon. But even in private we have never purposely degraded one another. And, I can say truthfully that she has always supported me—without exception. I could not abide anyone attempting to hurt her, whether by word or deed. As any normal husband, I would immediately rise to her defense and her attackers would have to deal with me.

Now, if I being human and imperfect, seek to love and protect my bride, how much more does the Lord watch over us, His bride? The Body of Christ is the apple of His eye, and He will vigorously protect us.

"For thus says the LORD of hosts: 'He sent Me after glory, to the nations which plunder you; for he who touches you touches the apple of His eye'" (Zechariah 2:8).

When considering the complex community we call a local church, it is easy to understand how judgment and criticism often prevail. But I want to remind you that the Church belongs, first and foremost, to her Bridegroom—the Lord. We should never sit as naysayers, attacking her or demeaning her—within or outside the doors of the church. God has called us to unity, acceptance, and grace. Does that mean we can never criticize a particular church or pastor? Think about it this way—whoever those people are, whomever that pastor is, they are first of all His bride. Any negative discussion about them should first take place between you and their Bridegroom. If it needs to go any further, it must be wrapped in humble respect, considering with Whom you're really dealing.

When we come against the Church,
we are poking our finger in God's eye.
Not a prospect I would
like to consider.

A FRIEND OF THE BRIDEGROOM

Personally, I want to be a friend of the Bridegroom. The friend of the bridegroom was to care for the bride and make sure her every need was met so that she would be prepared for the day when the bridegroom came to take her home. This friend was a trusted person, someone the groom could count on. The friend would never take advantage of, or in any way hurt, the bride.

John the Baptist saw himself as such a man: *"He who has the bride is the bridegroom; but the friend of the bridegroom, who stands and hears him, rejoices greatly because of the bridegroom's voice. Therefore this joy of mine is fulfilled"* (John 3:29).

Jesus also saw John as such a man: *"...What did you go out into the wilderness to see? A reed shaken by the wind? But what did you go out to see? A man clothed in soft garments? Indeed, those who wear soft clothing are in kings' houses. But what did you go out to see? A prophet? Yes, I say to you, and more than a prophet. For this is he of whom it is written: 'Behold, I send My messenger before Your face, Who will prepare Your way before*

*You.' Assuredly, I say to you, among those born of women there
has not risen one greater than John the Baptist; but he who is least
in the kingdom of heaven is greater than he"* (Matthew 11:7-11).

John saw the big picture. He knew his role as friend of the
Bridegroom and he didn't deviate from it. He honored his Lord by
being faithful and preparing a way for Him.

OUR ROLE TODAY

Too often I have heard people readily chime in to put down the
Church. Glaring faults and uncovered sin has made the Body of
Christ a target for such ridicule. Not long ago I was with a group of
indignant ministry leaders who were sharing their experiences with
various churches and pastors. They vented with arrogance about
the way they had been treated. When I observed their attitude, it
was no wonder to me that pastors had rejected them—it was an
attempt to protect their churches!

Good pastors are also friends of the Groom. They are attempting to prepare the bride for His coming, attending to her needs
until He arrives. The local church is one of God's chosen means by
which He is moving on the earth today. Churches have flaws, and
do not always behave properly, but they are a part of His bride.
Consider the price He paid to redeem her:

*"Who gave Himself for us, that He might redeem us from ev-
ery lawless deed and purify for Himself His own special people,
zealous for good works"* (Titus 2:14).

Surprisingly, it is often the flawed and rough-edged people of
the local church that God uses the most to grow us up into mature
people of faith. When I was a young boy, I collected rocks. I was
fascinated with the idea that I could make them smooth and color-
ful. To do this, I followed a design and made a cage into which
water would flow. The cage moved round and round because of a

pulley linked to an electric motor. Over time, the stones became shiny and smooth because they rubbed against each other. The Church is similar. We rub each other smooth!

While I fully recognize that the Body of Christ is infinitely bigger in scope than the local church, I want pastors to understand the full significance of their role, regardless of the size of the congregation, and not to limit God in any way.

We must respect the bride and humbly serve her whether in the local church, or in the other numerous places God has positioned His Body. Preparing her for His coming means that she will be clean and dressed in white. The ministry of deliverance fulfills that vision. The time is now. The Groom is coming soon. We must make the bride ready for His arrival.

May God bless you as you seek to make yourself and His bride ready.

Part Three

A
PERSONAL
STORY

A sandbag makes a strange altar. Yet, at that moment in Vietnam, a coarse, dusty bag had suddenly become holy ground. For the first time in my life, I encountered the living God. I say *living*, for until that time I had created my own image of God. Now my life, and my self-made god, were falling apart.

It was a strange surrounding for such a meeting. I sat motionless on a wall of sandbags that bordered the 504th Military Police Battalion just outside the city of Qui Nhon, Vietnam. It was monsoon season, 1967. Sitting there at ten o'clock at night, it seemed my world was collapsing from within. I had done a lot of talking about God—but had certainly never really known Him. What brought me to this strange place at this awful time? How did I end up here—like this?

My thoughts went back to England, where I was born. Life was not easy in England in 1946. World War II had just ended, and there was great rejoicing among the weary, but grateful, people. My father, who had been recently discharged from the Royal Navy, was with his dying father at a hospital. My mother went into labor and walked three miles to the hospital in Orpington to give birth. After I was born, she had a vision of my grandfather standing at her bedside. He said, "One is taken and another is born." A few hours later my father came in to be with her. Of course, he didn't have to say a word. She knew his father was gone. I was born the very day my grandfather died.

Other memories began to surface as I sat upon my makeshift altar in Southeast Asia reflecting on my life. As a little boy of five, I attended the Anglican Church with my parents every Sunday. One particular Sunday the rector was preaching about devotion to God when he said, "How many of you would be bold enough to come forward to declare your love for your Heavenly Father?" His question was rhetorical, but to a five-year old it made no differ-

ence. I knew I wanted to express my love for my Father in Heaven.
I stepped out of the pew and went straightway to the front of the
church by the podium. The rector was surprised to see me come
forward, and I was embarrassed to notice that I was the only one who
took his remarks seriously. I began to cry as the congregation chuck-
led at the cute little lad. For them, it was cute—but for me, it was
intensely serious.

No one could have had better parents than I had. They had known
each other since they were five years old. Their numerous, wonder-
filled stories of growing up fed the awe and love we held in our
hearts for them—my father teaching Churchill's daughters to drive a
car, my mother putting on little plays with the grandchildren of
Charles Dickens. My mother was eighteen and my father was twenty-
one when they came forward during an evangelistic tent meeting
that had come into town. Two years later they married.

Dad was a quiet, strong man. His eyes were kind and gentle.
When necessary they could also stop me in my tracks. He was honorable, brave, and a man of great integrity. He distinguished himself
while serving in the Royal Navy, by being awarded the Distinguished
Service Medal (the highest award given to an enlisted man), the Distinguished Service Cross, (the highest award given to him after becoming an officer working as a Commando), and the Croix de Guerre
(awarded to him by Charles DeGaulle for his work with the French
Underground). A boy could not have had a better dad. I have included his brief testimony of his war experiences in the appendix of
this book.

My mother is also a person of great strength and character. She
had survived the bombings of London, and raised my older brother
and sister alone while my dad was off at war.

My mother herself was a child prodigy. At the age of five, she
sat down at the piano and began to play a piece of music she had

heard from memory. Her parents noticed her incredible gift and enabled her to have music lessons. She would go on to receive an Associate and Licentiate from the London College of Music. She played as an accompanist at the School of Ballet in London, and eventually earned another degree from the Royal Academy of Dance in classical ballet. I remember going with her to the Academy and sitting under the piano as she played for the ballet students. Two things were set in stone during that time: my love for classical music and my commitment to never dance ballet!

Our home was happy and filled with pleasant memories. My mother made the home gentle, loving, and full of laughter. Dad made the home safe and full of adventure. In 1998, he went home to be with the Lord. He was the best friend I ever had. My mother continues to be a loving and godly inspiration to our entire family.

HIDDEN DANGER OVERSEAS

When I was seven, our family moved to Canada. Our relatives did not receive this very well, since no Hayward from our family had left England. In fact, my aunt wouldn't speak with Dad for two years after that, branding him a deserter of the Crown. But we all survived and settled down just outside Toronto. What days those were for me! I found adventures at every turn. I especially loved winter—ice-skating to school, making snowmen, doing flips in the snow-covered ditches, building snow forts, and having snowball fights with my friends. (Dad recalled the winter in a different way. He recalled trying to get his car out of the snow-covered ditches, scraping ice off the walkway, and trying to open frozen door locks.)

Something tragic took place in Canada, too, something imperceptible at the time. My parents drifted away from fellowship with other believers. In England we were active in a church; in Canada we were not. Though I grew up in a truly loving home, we lacked foundational instruction about the gospel of Jesus Christ. As time went on, my family paid a price for the absence of biblical knowledge. Thankfully, we all have since come to know and accept the love and grace of God through the gift of His dear Son. He truly is our Redeemer.

We left Canada after four and a half years and journeyed to California. I was eleven. We somehow made it there in a 1949 Ford. It was fully loaded. What I mean by that is that it held my mother and father, my sister, my dog Boots, a TV set in the trunk, along with luggage, and me. Traveling along the famous Route 66, we survived breakdowns in Mississippi and tornados in Texas, and somehow made it to the Golden State.

We settled in the city of Lakewood. By the time Dad found work, we were surviving on dimes and nickels found under the couch cushions. We began attending a little Congregational church where I made several friends. We did all the "church" things—Sunday worship, choir, Sunday School, potlucks, etc.—but there was a deep void in my soul. No one ever talked about eternal life, heaven and hell, witnessing for Jesus. In fact, the Bible was not really considered relevant. This hunger for a spiritual connection continued to grow in me, though I found no answers in that place.

TWO IMPORTANT FORESHADOWINGS

When I was fourteen, I approached my father, knowing he had traveled the world extensively, and said, "Dad, I would like to spin a globe and wherever my finger touches, I would like to go there." My father said, "OK, son, spin it." With the two of us gently leaning over the small, brown world, I spun the globe then placed down my finger randomly. "There, Dad. That's where I want to go." My father looked at where my finger had stopped the globe from spinning and said, "No, son. You don't want to go there. There will be trouble someday and it won't be a safe place to go." "But Dad, that's where I'm going. Vietnam! I'm going to go to Vietnam, Dad." Little did I know that is exactly where I would end up—in Vietnam, on this sandbag, having an encounter with the living God.

Another unforgettable event took place that same year. It was a warm summer day. My father was preparing some hamburgers outside on the grill. I was standing next to my mother when she said, "Chris, I want to tell you about something that happened to me before you were born. Your father had just come home for a few days leave from the war in 1945. We were walking by Winchester Cathedral when we heard the most beautiful singing. It was so captivating that we went in and sat down. While sitting there enthralled, I felt as if I were caught up to heaven—I was so close to the Lord. In that moment He somehow communicated to me that I was going to have a special child, and that he would be an influence for good in the world. When I told your father what had happened, he said that it was impossible for me to know I was pregnant since he had only been home a few days. I told him that I *knew* and was absolutely certain because of what the Lord had said. You are that child, Chris." I pondered that conversation for a long time. A sense of destiny took hold of me. Even today, I occasionally look back and wonder.

THE SET-UP

About this time, I began working. First, I had a paper route, then I did door-to-door sales. From there I became a clerk for a department store, and eventually ended up working at Christopher's Body Shop. It was at this point that my life took a decisive turn. Having little biblical foundation, but a great desire to understand spiritual things, I was an easy target for deception. When a person seeks to understand spiritual things, but the Church will not speak, another voice—a more sinister one—will.

Mrs. Christopher had inherited the paint and body shop from her deceased husband. She ran it well. I was hired as "gopher"—someone to go for this and go for that. One week, while cleaning out her bookcases, I noticed all sorts of interesting books. She had books on reincarnation, mental telepathy, astrology, etc. It wasn't long before she had a student keen to listen. She was a Rosicrucian, a mystical order that slowly draws people into increasing association and activity with the occult. Before long I also became a Rosicrucian. I wanted to know more about spiritual things, so I sought any activity where a more direct contact with the spirit realm was possible. I found such a place in Long Beach, California. Twice a week I would travel down to Joshua's Temple to learn how I could become a medium, someone who linked the spiritual world with the earthly, human world. This now had become my life's ambition.

JOSHUA'S TEMPLE

It was an old, large, single-story home with a large parlor where services were conducted. We would meet twice a week, Sunday and Wednesday evenings. Sundays were for the general public. Steven, a medium, would stand behind the pulpit, go into a trance, whereupon Joshua (presumed to be the Joshua of the Bible) would take possession of his body and speak through him (this is known as "channeling" today). I didn't recognize it as occultic or evil. I thought I was finally hearing truth about spiritual matters. I was fascinated by everything and wanted to be able to do it myself. Wednesdays were by invitation only. It was reserved for the few that wanted more. I was the perfect candidate. A small group of about eight would sit in a circle as Steven would go into a trance and channel several different "personalities."

A couple of times I was bothered by what I heard and saw. One evening, a spirit calling himself Jesus manifested. A newcomer in the group asked a question of it. She said, "Are you the Jesus of the Bible?" The response shocked me. "What does it matter if I am that Jesus," he shouted, " you need to listen to me!" I thought, *Wow. Why did that question bother him so much?*

A few weeks later, Steven confided in me that he tried to leave Joshua's Temple and give everything up. He was driving in the mountains when his car went out of control and rolled down an embankment. Steven walked away from the accident unscathed but was told by the spirits not to do that again. He was trapped. Again I thought, *If this is supposed to be good, why does it appear so bad?* Now I know that these were nothing more than demonic spirits taking possession of a willing vessel to teach demonic doctrine to deceive. At the time, I saw nothing evil about it all and aspired to greater abilities. I was in—hook, line, and sinker, actively seeking the world of the occult. I believed in it strongly, and was so zealous that I would have died for what I believed.

In my enthusiasm, I drew my parents into the Rosicrucian cult. They followed out of ignorance, unaware of the enemy's schemes. I am glad to say that a few years later they would renounce it all for a vibrant relationship with the Lord. They would also leave the nominal church they had attended for one that believed in the Word of God and taught it well.

YOU'RE IN THE ARMY NOW

At the age of eighteen, on Christmas Day, I surprised my parents by telling them I had joined the Army. It was 1964. My basic training took place at Ft. Polk, Louisiana. After that, I received specialized training at Ft. Benjamin Franklin in Indianapolis, Indiana. I was trained as a Personnel Specialist. Within a few weeks, my orders sent me to White Sands Missile Range, New Mexico. My basic duties were simple enough, and I was enjoying other activities as well. I had begun flight training prior to joining the Army and found a way to continue it at White Sands. I also landed a job at the base pool as a lifeguard during the summer months. Life was pretty good—until I received new orders. It seemed that I was about to be transferred to an outpost in the middle of the desert away from all my enjoyable activities. I couldn't allow this to happen. As a matter of policy, the base chaplain would conduct an orientation meeting for all new personnel. He explained that he was in need of a Chaplain's Assistant. I felt that I could fool him with enough spiritual lingo to convince him I'd make an excellent assistant and have my orders changed. He was convinced of my spirituality (so much for discernment), and then convinced the general to have my orders changed.

Each evening I would go into the Fort Chapel and conduct my meditations with candles, etc. I was a chaplain's assistant and as lost as a rock. The Lord has interesting ways of getting our attention. I thought I had pulled a fast one—but the Lord would have the last word. Week after week I was required to listen to the Word of God. On Sunday evenings we showed a film series designed to convince skeptics of the reality of God. The Lord was beginning to plow up the ground of my heart.

VIETNAM BOUND

Three months later new orders arrived. I was going to Vietnam. My father's prediction had come true. Vietnam *had* become the hotspot of the world—and a very dangerous place. I arrived in 1966. The war was in full swing. My duties were to assist the assigned chaplain and to protect him. He was not allowed to carry a weapon, but I was. Attached to the Military Police, we traveled over thirty thousand miles on the roads of Vietnam, running convoys to Pleiku, An Khe, and other towns.

One day we received news that the USO Tour was coming to Qui Nhon. Bob Hope and his entourage would set up at the airport, and Billy Graham would be attending. I had the privilege of meeting Dr. Graham, along with the Chief of Chaplains. As his plane pulled up, a jeep carrying Bob Hope also pulled up to greet him. It was quite a sight to watch the antics of Bob Hope as he kidded with Dr. Graham. When all the excitement faded, I introduced myself to the gentle man of God whose warm acceptance radiated with the love of God. He gripped my hand and then just gazed at me. At that moment, it was as if he and I were the only ones there. His eyes were kind and penetrating. I couldn't get the meeting out of my mind.

DISCOVERED!

Two weeks later, I was in the home of a missionary. Paul Travis and his wife had been in Vietnam for over forty-two years. They had been through the Japanese occupation, the French occupation, and now the American occupation of this small but strategic country. This godly couple had been instrumental in establishing a number of churches throughout the land. He was highly respected, and I was grossly ignorant. I was a chaplain's assistant—and still as lost as a rock. Since the age of fourteen, my life's ambition was wrapped up in the occult and becoming a medium. Being fairly well-versed, I gave a lesson to Mr. Travis, thinking he could learn from my vast experience and knowledge. For almost thirty minutes, he somehow endured my endless nonsense. I sat on his counter while he cut vegetables in his little home in Qui Nyon. He was getting a lesson on reincarnation, the necessity of karma, and spiritism. I was teaching him all about the great teachers and thinkers of our time. Finally he'd had enough. He put down his knife, looked at me and said, "What a shame!" Shocked, I replied, "What do you mean, 'What a

shame!'?" He simply responded, "You don't believe in a personal God, do you?" With one simple remark I was undone. No
Scripture, no sermon—just one simple question.

For two weeks his words rocked me. All my life I had been
yearning to know God. I knew there had to be something or Someone. From that moment of reckoning, I had felt like a bucket full
of holes, and whatever I tried to fill it with quickly flowed out.
And there was no end to the possibilities because there were very
few limits on my life. The security of feeling like I had everything
figured out evaporated. My head and my heart were corrupt, and I
was empty inside.

Now, sitting on that sandbag wall around the perimeter of the
504th Military Police Battalion, I was at the end of myself. Despite my extensive pursuit of spirituality, I had never spoken *with*
God before. Prayer had been all about me, and I did the talking.
Now, God had something to say. And in the presence of His infi-
nite holiness, a mirror was put up to my life. All the ugliness, the
entire facade was there. My belief system was empty—it just
wouldn't hold up under the strain of this *real* life. God gave me a
choice that night: I was invited to embrace His Son, Jesus Christ,
or choose to forever walk the path I currently traveled. I recall
running into the chapel tent, falling on my knees and crying out,
"Jesus, Jesus." At the time, that was the depth of my theological
understanding. I needed Jesus, and He came in. Now my Christian walk began.

PRAYERS OF THE FAITHFUL

Who was praying for my salvation? I knew of no one. My parents certainly prayed for me. They prayed for health and a safe
return, but not for my salvation. It wouldn't be until some year
later that I would discover the answer.

My wife, Karen, was in her seventh grade Sunday School class when her teacher said to all of the girls, "How many of you are praying for your husbands?" Well, of course this was met with giggles and questions of how could they do such a thing when they didn't even know who their husbands would be. She answered, "That's true. You don't know—but God does. You should be praying for him every day." Karen took her assignment quite seriously. From that moment on, every day of her life she has prayed for me. Two weeks into this new venture, the Lord spoke to her heart and said, "You're praying for him as if he knew Me. He doesn't!" At that point Karen began to pray, "Lord, make him miserable until he comes to know You." God answered her prayers. I was miserable.

All those prophecies, promises, and prayers converged upon me on that monsoon evening in Vietnam.

FIRST STEPS

It wasn't easy learning this new way of faith. For years I had opposed Christianity. I held many falsehoods and misconceptions that had to be set right, so I dove into the Word. The chaplain I was serving at the time was a good man, and he sought to help me in my new walk. One month after my conversion, he arranged to have me baptized in the South China Sea. I can't say it was a normal baptism. Most people being baptized aren't surrounded with men carrying M-16s to protect you. In three months I was to return home and be discharged from the Army. I had served 15 months in Vietnam.

My parents had, by this time, joined First Baptist Church of Lakewood, and were on fire for the Lord. It was a strong, Bible-believing church, so when I returned home it became my church as well. I have always appreciated the strong grounding in the Word of God that I received while attending there. It was also there where I met my wonderful wife. We were married in December of 1970.

THE SHADOW OF DEATH

Satan doesn't let go easily. Karen and I were living in Costa Mesa. I had left the banking world as branch manager of a savings and loan to work with Hal Lindsey and Chuck Missler in a publishing venture. During this time, I met Walter Martin and was able to travel with him for two years taping his lectures. Walter was the author of *The Kingdom of the Cults* (Bethany House), and was an expert in exposing erroneous doctrines.

It happened while I was at home one night. I awakened at five in the morning to go to the bathroom. When I returned to bed, a dark shadowy figure appeared in the room. It was blacker than black. It stood about eight feet tall and came around to the foot of the bed. Most hideous of all, it brought with it the stench of hopelessness and despair. I knew immediately that it was demonic. It then began to fall forward over me. It felt as if a thousand pound weight had been placed on top of my body. I could neither breathe nor talk. I was completely immobilized. Death seemed just around the corner. For a few moments I had a taste of hell. It is total loneliness, despair, and hopelessness. Only the word, "Jesus," came to my thoughts. In my mind, I uttered His name heavenward. After a couple of minutes the spiritual darkness left. I was exhausted and scared. My pajamas were soaked with sweat. Karen and I prayed. Early the next morning I called Walter. He encouraged me and prayed for me to be bold and not give in to the enemy's parlor tricks to scare me into believing his power over me was unstoppable. That kind of event happened again a few weeks later but with no success, and I was beginning to learn about spiritual warfare.

THE SWORD THAT THE ENEMY DRAWS

As I reflect upon my life, I see that the Lord has taken me on a very curious route. I was with Vision House Publishing for five years where I served as vice president; then I received an invitation to work at Word Publishing in Waco, Texas. After five years I became vice president of the video department, having previously served as the marketing director for the publishing department. All this time, Karen and I had become quite active in a local church. The church leaders approached me to ask if I was interested in serving as the church administrator.

It seemed a divergent step from my present vocational course. I committed myself to prayer over the decision. When asking the Lord what He wanted me to do, He replied, "What do *you* want to do?" I said, "Lord, I thought you were supposed to tell me." The Lord was prompting me to discover the correct answer. It wasn't long before I realized that my greatest desire was to make a difference in the lives of others. Anyone can learn how to do marketing plans. I wanted to know that my life really counted for something.

Karen and I prayed much during these days. Words fail to express my appreciation for Karen throughout the years of our marriage. She continues to show such strength of character—willing to leave a place of relative comfort in order to walk the path the Lord has laid out for us.

When we first married, I was the branch manager of World Savings and Loan in Brentwood, California. Like most buildings of its sort, it was a place of prestige. It appeared that I had a solid future ahead of me. But I was miserable. Several times a week I would take my lunchtime to go down to a park overlooking the Santa Monica beach. Standing alone I would cry out to God, asking that He would open a door for ministry. By all accounts I should have been happy, but like many other Christians, I sought to serve Him in a more direct way. Hal Lindsey was writing his book *Satan Is Alive and Well and Living on Planet Earth* (Zondervan). We had a mutual friend that informed Hal that I was a businessman who had come out of the occult. One day he paid me a visit at my branch. We went out for lunch while he interviewed me as research for a portion of his book. I mentioned to Hal my longing to be involved in ministry, and he told me of a man by the name of Chuck Missler who was forming a company to reproduce teaching tapes by prominent communicators. Chuck and I met, and before long I was telling Karen that I felt God was opening a door for ministry. She thought she had married a banker—but now it seemed she had married a wild-eyed dreamer. Nevertheless, she prayed and stood by me as I moved out of the luxury of the savings and loan, and into a small hallway of a small office. My desk was a card table upon which a reel-to-reel tape deck was used for the purpose of editing tapes. We didn't know what we were doing at first, but we learned. And throughout all this, Karen was as solid as a rock.

During those early years of our marriage, I realize now how insensitive I was. By this time we had two small children. I would work long hours, leaving her isolated at home. We had only one car, and she had no place to go. It was only by God's grace and her great love that we endured. It is possible for people to compromise the very best things in life for the sake of "ministry." Ministry has eaten up many marriages and devoured many lives. I have told my staff at Cleansing Stream Ministries that people are more important than ministry. That may sound like an odd statement since ministry involves people. But too many marriages, too many children, have been sacrificed on the altar of spiritual work. I don't believe Jesus had this in mind. What many may call "sacrifice" might actually be self-serving and ego-building. We say it is for God, when it might actually be for us. Well, even through this, Karen never failed to bring peace to our home and sensibility to my life.

One Way Library was soon purchased by Vision House Publishers. I moved along with the company. Not long after that, an opportunity came to join Word Publishing in Waco, Texas. This would be the first time Karen had ever moved far away from her family. It was not easy, and took much faith. Her continued encouragement gave me strength and confidence. So, we sold our house, packed up, and drove off to wonderful Waco.

We must have looked odd driving in our 1970 Olds Ninety-Eight— "Old Blue" we called it. It had a tow-hitch on the back that pulled a Honda Civic. Seated in the Honda Civic were two dogs—a German Shepherd and a Collie. The German Shepherd liked to sit upright behind the wheel. Many passersby did double-

> There was a time when I was a weapon in the hands of the enemy. By God's grace He has saved and delivered me. Now, by that same grace, I will become a sword against our adversary.

takes on our shepherd! We encountered severe ice storms and a few other hazards along our way. But Karen never complained.

So, as I found myself seeking the Lord for an answer as to whether I should go to work at Highland Baptist Church as the church administrator, it was Karen who received a clear word from the Lord. It was, "Cast your net on the other side of the boat and you shall bring in a great haul." That Scripture has come to pass.

After a year, opportunities were given me to fill in for the pastor when he was out of town. Not long after that, I was ordained.

Four years later, our family left Texas for Mt. Vernon, Illinois, where I served as the founding pastor of Christian Fellowship Church. We began with five families and it grew healthily over the following eleven years. About midway through my term with Christian Fellowship, I became acquainted with Cleansing Stream. For over twelve years I had attended the pastoral leadership conferences sponsored by Dr. Jack Hayford at The Church on the Way in Van Nuys, California. It was there that I first heard about this ministry. But it wasn't until I was a pastor in Illinois that I took a serious look at it. An elder of my congregation and his wife were also made aware of The Cleansing Stream Seminar and asked if I would be willing to introduce it to our church. We agreed to begin first with four couples and see how it went. Since the Seminar included a ministry Retreat, we sent the elder and his wife to California to participate. They came back glowing with joy. The Lord had done much in their lives, as I could attest to.

Within a few months, we began to open it up to the whole church. Our next Seminar consisted of around sixty people. Many who didn't join were skeptical. I can recall a specific incident with a loving, but severely wounded woman in our church. She attended the Seminar and Retreat without her husband. He refused to get involved with this scary-sounding ministry. His wife was quite challenging in many respects. After the retreat she came home and asked her husband if she could wash his feet (literally). He was flabbergasted. A few days later he said to me, "Pastor, I want to sign up for the next one. If it could have such a dramatic impact on my wife, then it must be real. I want to go next!" In a few more months, over ninety percent of our congregation had been through the Seminar and Retreat.

Soon, we began The Cleansing Stream Discipleship Seminar, implementing prayer teams in the church. Within a year, I had thirty adults who were not only cleansed from strongholds in their lives, but also ready to serve alongside of me to do the work of the ministry. My people were being discipled and trained. No longer was I alone in ministry, but one among many who had a heart to serve God, bless others, and come alongside of me, their pastor. It was a rich experience, as it is a rare thing, especially in a church our size, to have so many trained people who wanted only to bless others and stand with their pastor. I became a believer in the effectiveness of Cleansing Stream Ministries and their two Seminars, and agreed to serve as their Regional Representative for the central part of the United States.

In 1998, Cleansing Stream Ministries went through a change of leadership, and I was asked to come and serve the ministry fulltime. That same year our family moved to California, and I joined Cleansing Stream Ministries where I now serve as president. Everything in life, it seems, prepared me for what I'm now doing. Finance and publishing have certainly played a role. But most of all, it was in the furnace of pastoral ministry where my life has been forged the most. It is here where my love for the local church, and those who serve in them, was born.

The book of Psalms says, *"Their sword shall enter their own heart, and their bows shall be broken"* (Psalm 37:15). The Scriptures promise that we will be able to use our enemy's own weapon against him. For this, I praise the Lord. There was a time when I was a weapon in the hands of the enemy. By God's grace He has saved and delivered me. Now, by that same grace I will become a sword against our adversary.

Appendix One

I cannot adequately express the impact my father had—and continues to have—upon my life and ministry. To know him is to know a piece of my own heart and soul. For this reason, I have included an excerpt from a talk he gave at First Baptist Church in Lakewood, California. In this brief testimony, he summed up his war years. I hope you will find it as thought provoking and inspirational as I do.

TESTIMONY OF MY LIFE IN THE ROYAL NAVY
by
WILLIAM A. HAYWARD
July 5, 1993

I have been asked to give the testimony of my life in the Armed Services, and I am very honored to be asked to do so. I joined the British Royal Navy in 1941, and left the service in 1946, starting my career as a Petty Officer (E.R.A. Engine Room Artificer). When I left in 1946, I had reached the rank of Engineer Commander. This represents five short years of hectic activity in a seven-year, global war.

You know, Paul preached the gospel and suffered for it. I would remind you, that preaching the gospel *costs* something. Paul wrote:

"Are they ministers of Christ?—I speak as a fool—I am more: in labors more abundant, in stripes above measure, in prisons more frequently, in deaths often. From the Jews five times I received forty stripes minus one. Three times I was beaten with rods; once I was stoned; three times I was shipwrecked; a night and a day I have been in the deep; in journeys often, in perils of waters, in perils of robbers, in perils of my own countrymen, in perils of the Gentiles, in perils in the city, in perils in the wilderness, in perils in the sea, in perils among false brethren; in weariness and toil, in

sleeplessness often, in hunger and thirst, in fastings often, in cold and nakedness—besides the other things, what comes upon me daily: my deep concern for all the churches. Who is weak, and I am not weak? Who is made to stumble, and I do not burn with indignation? If I must boast, I will boast in the things which concern my infirmity. The God and Father of our Lord Jesus Christ, who is blessed forever, knows that I am not lying" (2 Corinthians 11:23-31).

What I have just read from the Bible, is what spreading the gospel costs. What I am going to tell you now is a minute part of what freedom costs.

I made a total of 16 trips across the North Atlantic Ocean on convoy duty, with three trips to Freetown, West Africa, two trips to North Africa off the Mediterranean, and one trip to Murmansk, Russia, the only port open during the winter months. That trip became known as the closest trip to hell. It was not misnamed.

Three of my ships were torpedoed, two of them in the South Atlantic. In the last nuance, I was blown out of the hole made by the torpedo. It happened at night, but I managed to find a Carley Raft (cork float) cast adrift from the ship. I climbed onto it, and hauled four other men on board. All were in pretty bad shape. When daylight came, there was not a sign of anything. The ship had gone down. We were the only survivors of a crew of 175 men.

Alone in the South Atlantic, we were at least 700 miles from land, with no food or water and nothing to protect us from the tropical sun. Three of my shipmates died from exposure. One went mad from drinking seawater and jumped overboard. I managed to survive by making myself a fishing line and using my own flesh as bait. I caught one fish and ate it raw.

I was picked up unconscious and completely dehydrated by a returning convoy and returned to England. By that time, I had recovered from my ordeal and was sent to a ship due to sail to the Mediterranean and Tobruk, North Africa. Upon returning from this trip, the ship was diverted to the Bay of Biscay. An Italian sub had escaped into the Bay and was attacking Allied shipping. Our orders were to find and destroy it. We did locate it and blew it to the surface. We took the crew on board and were told to try and take the sub back to Gibraltar.

I was sent on board with six men to attempt this. It was suspected that time-delayed explosive charges had been placed on the main sea valve to send the sub to the bottom. They were right. I found 2 charges: one on the sea valve, the other on the stem torpedo door. I ordered all men out and had just reached the conning tower when there was a tremendous explosion and the sub started to go down by the stem. I became jammed in the conning tower hatch and was twenty feet under when I broke loose and popped to the surface. I was picked up and went back to England.

On arrival there, I was informed that my commission had come through and that I had been appointed as Squadron Engineer to 26 Flack ships (antiaircraft ships). While I was on this assignment I was also informed that I would be working for Ml 5 (Intelligence). My job was to obtain information from the French Resistance regarding obstructions on the beaches off Arromanch on the Normandy Coast. Also, I was to coordinate air drops of necessary supplies of ammunition and explosives for their use in destroying road and rail traffic. All this was done under the eyes of the Germans. In preparation for an Allied landing in the future, I traveled to France by submarine and was rowed ashore by rubber boat 16 times before D-Day. All the information obtained I carried directly to Churchill and Eisenhower, and to the Chiefs of the Armed Forces—usually to their meeting in the Library at Chartwell, Churchill's country residence in Kent, England.

After the invasion of France, my next appointment was to the Far East—to India. I was informed when I arrived in Bombay that I was to report to the Military Governor in Peshawar. It seemed that an Afghanistan Mullah (a tribal chieftain), who was educated at Oxford University in England and was very pro-western, had vital information regarding the infiltrating of the Soviets into India. He would only convey this information to a representative of the British Government. I was chosen, but to this day I do not know why.

I was given a bodyguard of six men from the Gurka Rifles. They were wonderful mountainmen and fearless fighters. I had to meet this Afghan about 20 miles inside Afghanistan and 10,000 feet up in the Himalayan Mountains. We entered through the Khyber Pass. I was told not to get captured alive and was given a hard cyanide pill as a last resort. The mission was successfully completed. It was while I was in Peshawar that I had the good fortune to be introduced to Gandhi and Nehru at a soiree given for him by the governor. On arrival back in Bombay, I was told that my next assignment was to a ship patrolling off the Burma Coast in support of General Slim who was driving the enemy out of Burma. The ship's engineer had been taken very ill and had to be relieved. The ship was a turboelectric, with which I was familiar. It meant transshipping at sea, so I was sent aboard a freighter. We finally rendezvoused off the Burma Coast. The ship was at that time supplying fresh water from its evaporators to storage tanks set in the edge of the jungle.

While we were doing this, we were jumped by the enemy and marched off into the jungle. After several miles we stopped, and all six of us were tortured, forced to dig our own upright graves and then bayoneted until we jumped in. They had tied my right arm to a board and torn all my fingernails out with ordinary pliers. We were left in the sun with honey poured around our necks for the ants to eat. Two of my men were shot for screaming—two just died. I wished I could have died. The last thing I remember was calling out, "God, help me." He did. Two days later I was rescued by a patrol of General Slim's army. I was taken back to my ship that was waiting off the coast. My hands were treated, the swelling went down, but I could not use my right hand. However, by the time we arrived in Singapore it had improved. It was while my ship was having a boiler cleaned, that I was told that I had been appointed to the First Naval Mission to visit Nagasaki after the atom bomb had been dropped.

The devastation we saw as we flew over the city was indescribable. And when we actually visited the city the following day, I was physically sick. Those people who were moving around looked terrible. Some actually just lay down on the ground and died from radiation. I did not get away unharmed. My jaw was affected by radiation, which caused the lower part of my face to erupt in blisters. Ten years later it was necessary to remove all my teeth. The roots had curled upwards. As a result, I have no lower gums, and cannot bite an apple or chew anything hard. When I finally arrived back in England, I left the service.

I will conclude with this message, particularly to young people. We all strive to reach a position of responsibility in this life. I hope many of you will manage to do this. I would remind you, however, that becoming the president of a company, a commander in any of the armed services, a senior pastor of church, such as Pastor Ron, is, at times, a very lonely position which carries with it the sole responsibility of final decisions which will affect the lives of many people. Freedom is a very precious commodity that should be treasured above all else. All these can only be obtained with the help of Jesus Christ. I have called on Him many times, and He has never left or forsaken me. We should, at this time, remember all our armed services and ask God to preserve them and keep them strong, to enable them to protect our freedoms and those of other people who are in need.

Thank you for listening.

Appendix Two

ADDITIONAL RESOURCE

For further biblically sound treatment of the ministry of deliverance I recommend:

The Finger of God by Pastor Jack Hayford,
Living Way Ministries, 1993.

Appendix Three

CLEANSING STREAM MINISTRIES
CONTACT INFORMATION

Please feel free to contact Cleansing Stream Ministries for questions on the Resources, Seminars and Retreats mentioned in this book. You can reach us…

By Mail: Cleansing Stream Ministries
P. O. Box 7076
Van Nuys, CA 91409

By Phone: (800) 580-8190 (Toll free within the U.S.)
(818) 678-6888 (Local)

By Fax: (888) 580-8199 (Toll free within the U.S.)
(818) 678-6885 (Local)

Or visit our website: www.cleansingstream.org

We look forward to hearing from you.

Subject Index

A

abandonment, 29
Abraham, 16
abuse, 30-31, 95
accountability, 42, 45-46, 51, 54, 120
Acts 19:15, 45
angels, 96
anger, 28-30, 94, 95, 100-101
anointing oil, 106
authority, 18-19, 45, 54, 59, 61, 106-110, 120, 137
authority, stepping outside of, 59-60

B

body (human), 69-73
break, 105-106, 133

C

captivity, 24-26
changes, lifestyle, 113-114
Christian Fellowship Church, 162
Christopher's Body Shop, 151
1 Chronicles 4:9-10, 77
Church on the Way, The, 20, 28, 56, 162
Church, Early, 13-15, 23
church, local, 15-17
Churchill, Winston, 148
cleansing process, 79
Cleansing Stream Discipleship Seminar, 22, 40, 45-47, 50, 55-56, 83, 117, 119-127, 129, 131, 135, 138-140, 163
Cleansing Stream Discipleship Training Commitment Agreement, 126
Cleansing Stream Ministries, 8, 20, 21-23, 28, 36, 41, 44, 56, 82, 124, 140, 160, 162-163
Cleansing Stream Regional Retreat(s), 22, 23, 30, 37-38, 40, 45, 50, 51, 55, 57-60, 62-63, 68, 80, 81-98, 109-110, 112, 114, 116, 117, 123, 125, 131, 137, 139, 140, 162
Cleansing Stream Seminar, The, 22, 28, 29, 30, 41, 50, 55-56, 68, 80, 81-82, 93, 98, 102, 110, 112, 114, 117, 125, 130-131, 137, 139, 140, 162
Colossae, 43
Colossians 1:9-14, 43
Colossians 1:13, 15
commit to God, 74-75
confidentiality, 46-47, 125, 135
conscience, seared, 101-102
1 Corinthians 1:27, 56
1 Corinthians 6:19, 114
1 Corinthians 9:24-25, 65
1 Corinthians 13:4-7, 46
2 Corinthians 1:10, 6-7, 72
2 Corinthians 3:18, 73
2 Corinthians 4:2, 105
2 Corinthians 5:10, 95
2 Corinthians 10:4, 106
2 Corinthians 10:4-5, 99
2 Corinthians 11:23-31, 165
counseling, 59-60, 140-141
counterfeits, 129
curses, 104
Cyril of Jerusalem, 13-14

D

David, 40-41, 114
Dawson, Joy, 9
DeGaulle, Charles, 148
deliverance, definition of, 19
deliverance, maintaining, 51
demon possession, 19-20
demons, 12, 48, 52, 59, 61, 62-63, 76, 94, 109-110, 129
demons, Christians and, 19-20